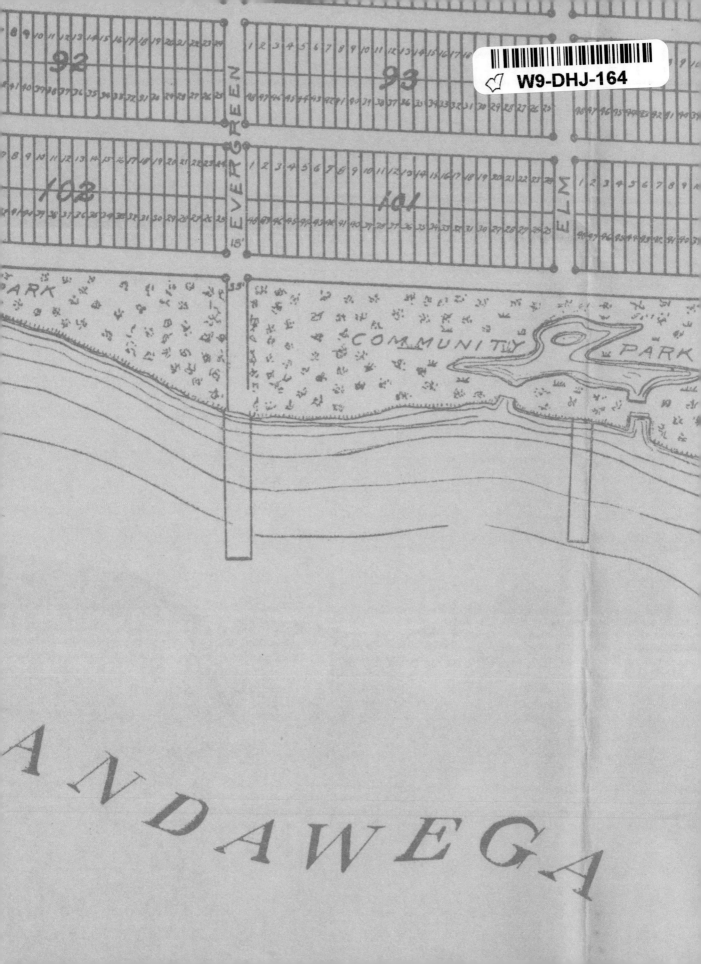

FOUND, FREE & FLEA

FOUND, FREE & FLEA

creating collections from vintage treasures

TEREASA SURRATT

Clarkson Potter/Publishers

NEW YORK

CLARKSON POTTER is a trademark and POTTER with colophon
is a registered trademark of Random House, Inc.

Library of Congress Cataloging-in-Publication Data
Surratt, Tereasa.
   Found, free & flea / Tereasa Surratt.—1st ed.
   1. Americana—Collectors and collecting.   2. Collectibles—United
States.   I. Title.
   NK805.S95   2011
745.1075—dc22   2010037179

ISBN 978-0-307-88529-6

Printed in China

Design by Stephanie Huntwork
Photograph credits appear on page 206
Jacket design by Stephanie Huntwork
Front jacket photograph by Tereasa Surratt

10 9 8 7 6 5 4 3 2

First Edition

FOR DAVID, CHARLIE & FRANKIE

CONTENTS

Introduction 8

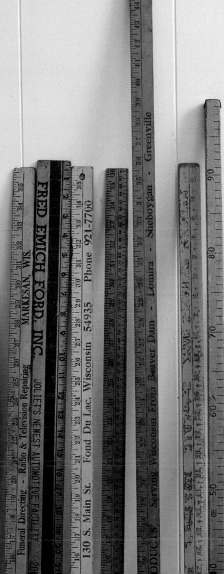

introduction

Imagine a rural hideaway with ninety years of forgotten and unwanted belongings locked away. Then one day you stumble on this place, someone gives you the key . . . and at once you uncover nine decades of once-loved possessions from generations past. It all started when my husband said he wanted us to buy his childhood Wisconsin summer camp, Wandawega Lake Resort—which had been a speakeasy, brothel, modest vacation resort, Catholic Church retreat, and summer camp. It was a lonely collection of orphaned cottages and decrepit buildings and all the forgotten stuff left within them. With much persuading, he convinced me to go back just one more time to see the place with its caved ceilings and raccoon squatters. As we were making our way through, curious little items kept popping up: a single Depression era glass bowl, an engraved trophy, an embroidered hankie with someone's initials. They were little reminders of happier times— at some point in their lives, they had clearly been precious to someone. As we dug through attics, cellars, basements, and crawl spaces, these clues kept dropping in our path.

The many lives of this place began to reveal themselves through the abandoned possessions of former occupants. The first discovery was a tiny orange canvas life vest in a box in the attic. Months later, an old family photo album surfaced prominently featuring a photo of my husband, forty years earlier, proudly wearing that little vest. Every discovery raised more questions. What happened to this china set's matching brothers and sisters? (It likely had dutifully survived

OPPOSITE The Camp Wandawega map of the grounds, illustrated by our friend Jon.

fifty-plus years of meatloaf dinners, a few generations of kids, and several house moves.) Was its destiny really to end up here, in an attic, under piles of debris hosting a family of mice? That is when our mission started. When we adopted this neglected place, it marked the beginning of a very long undertaking to resurrect the buildings, the history, and, most of all, the collections, while honoring the humble origins of this place by doing it all on the cheap, following the self-imposed rule of *found, free, or flea*. This is the story of thriftiness and a determination to transform discarded objects into more than 150 full collections again—a testament that collecting doesn't take much money, just a love of the forgotten, everyday things that got left behind.

LEFT Two of the early proprietors, circa 1950s

BELOW The beginning of our resurrection, 2007

11

step 1
finding treasures in the attics

step 2
resurrecting the collections through found, free, or flea

step 3
displaying, using, and living with collections for the cottage, cabin, and camp

a camp's life past eras, former occupants, and those who left it all behind at wandawega lake resort

ERA 1: BLIND PIG

1926

SPEAKEASY

Chicagoans seeking to capitalize on the opportunity presented by Prohibition build "Wandawega Hotel"

1929

ORGANIZED CRIME

The place was outfitted for the distribution of liquor, gun running, and gambling, including multiple exits, trapdoors, and hidden hatches to conceal stockpiles.

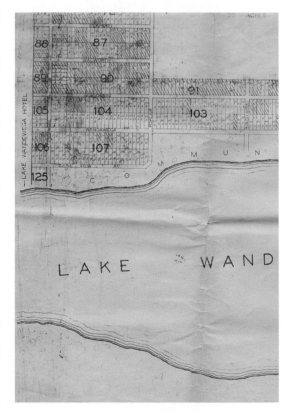

1930

HOUSE OF ILL REPUTE

Although Prohibition would come to an end in 1933, the demand for "ladies of the night" would not. Wandawega Hotel remained a discreet place where the world's oldest profession could continue to thrive. "Little Orphan Annie's Bar"—named after the madame herself—became a popular hangout for everyone, from the local law enforcement to Chicagoans looking for the company of the ladies.

1939

CABINS

Over the decades, a series of cabins was added to provide additional accommodations for guests. The restaurant and bar (pictured here), called "Little Orphan Annie's," was a local favorite.

1950s

LAKE RESORT, BAR & RESTAURANT

By 1951, the place finally goes legit when it's renamed Wandawega Lake Resort by its new owners, a Chicago-area Polish family. With the "ladies of the night" banished, the modest resort bar becomes an idyllic getaway for working-class Chicagoans looking for a convenient, affordable retreat. The bar remains open and serves as a popular hangout for the growing "year-round" community.

1961

THE CATHOLIC CHURCH

In 1961, the property is purchased by the Latvian Marian Fathers, a Catholic Order of priests, who bless the property and move in a reliquary and other sacred vessels. Unable to return to Latvia due to the Soviet occupation, Latvian priests who fled war-torn Europe intend to turn "Vandavega" into their retirement home.

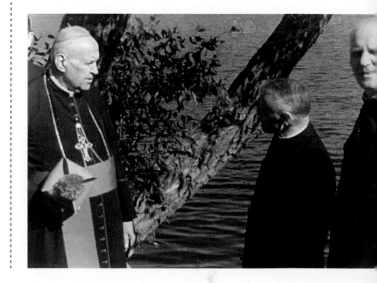

1972

LATVIAN CHURCH CAMP

The old resort becomes a summer gathering place for Midwest Catholic Latvians seeking to maintain a sense of community some 4,500 miles from their native land. The industrious moms organize an informal kids camp every summer for their children, complete with swimming, hiking, fishing, crafts, campfires, and a morning flag-raising followed by "calisthenics." My husband (pictured below, second boy from right) and his family spent all of his childhood summers there.

2004

RESURRECTION BEGINS

With Latvian independence in full swing, the Vatican instructs the Marian Fathers to sell the retreat and return to Latvia. By purchasing it, we keep the property "in the family" and restoration begins—a labor of love that continues to this day. We begin to uncover collectibles from every chapter of the old camp's many lives.

CAMP WANDAWEGA: THEN AND NOW—
SAME PLACE, DIFFERENT TIME

1

COLLECTED
FROM THE
KITCHEN

baking, burning,
gossiping over the stove

I t started with a hot pad. An unremarkable, four-by-four inch square of quilted cotton. The kind some Midwestern house-wife would have gotten as a Christmas freebie with her gas bill in a postwar farm town. We found the first one under a stove in one of the camp's many kitchens. It was an artifact from a forgotten era of '57 Chevys, diners, and Hank Williams. In the same kitchen, we would uncover an earthenware crock, a Deco-era rolling pin, and a Bakelite-handled spatula. All antiques—now collectibles—each with its own story.

Not surprisingly, the modern, plastic "dollar store" versions of spatulas don't offer the same charm as wooden ones. And everybody knows that cookie batter just somehow tastes better when sampled with a vintage wooden spoon. It brings back memories of sitting in Grandma's kitchen and watching her make homemade rhubarb jam and preserves in those lovely blue-tinted Ball jars. My grandma used the same jars, year in and out, for decades. It was a summertime ritual. Straining the fruit, melting the wax, sealing the jars—a tedious process that required patience and time. Because of my time spent in that kitchen, that's what comes to mind now when I come across a vintage can opener. It gives you an entirely new appreciation for how unbelievably easy we've

OPPOSITE We found the motherlode of Fiesta Ware in the old lodge kitchen. An early Homer Laughlin company brochure listing items available in the Fiesta line exclaims, "COLOR! That's the trend today . . . It gives the hostess the opportunity to create her own table effects . . . Plates of one color, Cream Soups of another, contrasting Cups and Saucers . . . it's FUN to set a table with Fiesta!"

got it. The summer camp had one main kitchen, and three smaller ones called guest-sharing kitchens. Eleven percolator coffeepots, six fly swatters, a dozen hand-crocheted pot holders, stacks and stacks of dishes—it was a virtual treasure trove of forgotten kitchen antiques. But my all-time favorite find was discovering a wall of paneling, behind which was hidden shelving that contained an extensive collection of Early California and Fiesta Ware. Why in God's name would someone panel over shelves still full of dishes? Was it intended as temporary storage, with intentions of returning later on to add access doors? Whatever the reason, the boarding-up had preserved the stacks, and we felt like we'd just hit the holy grail: more than a hundred pieces, in a variety of colors. What made the find even more special was the photograph that surfaced years later showing all of those lovely pieces proudly on display in the dining room of the restaurant in the 1950s. But not everything was discovered in its original set. The majority of the items were not, necessitating a scavenger hunt to find objects of a similar kind to reassemble collections—all of which would be displayed, and used, at the camp.

LEFT A photograph taken in the lodge restaurant of the owner (right) and his daughter. The cake stand is now on display in the main kitchen.

OPPOSITE Pulling off the vintage-kitchen look requires a retro tablecloth, enamelware, and at least one vintage rolling pin. What this teeny kitchen lacks in cable TV, it makes up in character.

cover yourself God bless the housewives, who changed out table linens daily in a season/theme/occasion-appropriate linen. We literally unearthed stacks of linens when we cracked open the doors of a metal linen cabinet, and I've been hooked ever since. My source for filling out the collection has primarily been flea markets. At any good-sized flea, you'll typically find at least a couple of linen vendors and a good number of regular dealers who have a trunk or two to dig through.

TOWELS—NOT JUST FOR TEA ANYMORE

Food, shelter, and vintage tablecloths: the three necessities for idyllic camp, cabin, or country chic.

LEFT In one of the guest kitchens, we use an old telescoping drying rack to display an assortment of vintage tea towels, dish towels, and tablecloths.

hint

While our antique fridges hardly qualify for an Energy Star rating, we use them only on those occasional weekends when the main kitchen fridge is on overload. While I'm a huge fan of vintage appliances—from stoves, to fridges, to fans—they're not for everyone. If you're going to give them serious use, you're better off with newer, safer, more energy efficient versions.

DAYS OF THE WEEK LINENS

Isn't it quaint to think that the average "ideal" 1950s housewife set out a different towel each day of the week? A set that we display was handmade by a very dear old friend we called Nana—it's a nice way to honor the memory of people and crafts of a bygone era when you use something that's been made by hand.

BELOW RIGHT A charming detail from one of the "days of the week" dish towels made by Nana.

ABOVE Made popular midcentury, tourist hand towels spiced up a kitchen and reminded folks of their vacations. We found only one ratty remnant of a tourist towel at Wandawega, but it set me off on a crazed search for more. This one hails from the Wisconsin Walworth County flea market—the most amazing source for all things country.

Hanging pot holders in a
geometric grouping on
simple hooks makes for a
dramatic display and
ensures there's always
one within arm's reach.

LEFT Here, a combination
of green, white, and yellow
hand-crocheted pot hold-
ers and hot pads are sim-
ply hung on a vintage coat
rack, with a couple of similarly hued vintage aprons.
It's an instant kitchen
"installation" that adds
charm and a splash of
color, and it's completely
functional as well.

fact
Besides the hand-
crocheted variety,
we found many pot
holders branded with
advertising logos
from local merchants.
These were apparently
popular giveaway items,
allowing businesses
to stay "top of mind,"
as postwar, post-
Depression housewives
were unlikely to throw
away anything of value,
even if the item was
covered in logos!

HOW TO GET YOUR OWN HAND-CROCHETED HOT PAD COLLECTION

If you're like me, every time you use vintage pot holders or hot pads, you'll feel the good karma of the little-old-lady hands that made them many moons ago, as well as all the folks who depended on them over the years.

By now, you're noticing a theme for starting a vintage collection:

STEP 1: Visit your neighborhood junk stores, garage sales, and Grandma's kitchen.

STEP 2: Find cheap, plentiful, and country-chic assortments of everyday items like hand-knit pot holders.

STEP 3: Edit them down to similarly colored, shaped, or textured collections that can be displayed easily— and used. Simple as that.

SOURCE YOUR OWN

- At garage sales and thrift shops. Expect to pay fifty cents to a buck apiece.
- Online (eBay, Etsy). You could spend up to five or ten bucks per.
- At Grandma's. She'll probably let them go for a hug, if you promise to give them a good home.

at your service We discovered the
first cake stand in a trunk in the farthest
possible corner of an attic. That would
be the beginning of a vast collection of
beautiful server ware we'd assemble from
yard sales and thrift stores over the next few
years, including over a dozen pitchers that I
augmented with some thrift finds. Although
our collection is of various styles and eras, a
common color scheme holds it all together.

These guys don't get a day
off; we use pitchers and
teapots for everything
from flower arrangements
to watering cans to, yes,
even beverage containers
on occasion.

PLATING PIES

We use a rustic farmhouse cabinet to display a set of the original restaurant plates we found boxed up in the attic. Also stored in this farmhouse cupboard: vintage pie tins that make great serving trays for pastries, cocktails, candies—even as dinner dishes for a fresh country look. It was common for bakeries to emboss their name into their pie tins (some bakeries even had a ten-cent deposit on each tin so the customers had an incentive to return to the bakery). These homely but awesome pieces of Americana can be had for as little as a few bucks each. But, like most antiques, be prepared to pay much more for rare and collectible tins.

hint

Restaurant plates are virtually indestructible—and quite heavy. If you'd like to find a complete set of your own, check out poshchicago.com, the website for the Chicago store P.O.S.H. From a vintage silver-plate tea service once used in an English country inn to a beautiful water pitcher from a grand hotel in New York, many of their tableware pieces tell a romantic story of an age gone by. But be forewarned: I've never been able to escape that store without spending less than two hours perusing the wares.

BELOW Proof of the strength of an old-school diner mug: in a pinch, you can actually use one to drive a large nail into a two by four. (It's true. Try it, but only with a genuine diner mug, or you'll have a fast mess on your hands.)

WHY DO THE COFFEE MUGS IN DINERS HAVE CONCAVE SIDES?

1 To minimize the volume of the cup
2 So it's easier to hold
3 For stability on a tray
4 For resistance to being knocked over
5 To make the space between the mug and the handle bigger
6 Perhaps to increase the mug's strength, as some have hypothesized

PUTTING IT OUT THERE

An antique country kitchen cupboard with glass doors is both practical and lovely to use in a dining room. It's the perfect piece of furniture for storing and displaying collections, inside and on top. The open shelves and glass-front cabinets keep you honest (there's no hiding messy assortments of junk here).

I love including mismatched chairs around a table: individual chairs are inexpensive to acquire at garage sales and flea markets (and yes, even in alleyways and beside Dumpsters if you are adventurous). All it takes is a serious hose-down, some wood glue, and fifteen minutes with a can of spray paint to unify and transform them from trash to a dining room suite.

RIGHT This cupboard sits in the main dining room, displaying an assortment of server ware and tablecloths ready to grace the table at a moment's notice.

LEFT Another view of the main dining room. A vintage "coffin table" found a second life as a carpenter's work table—as evidenced by the numerous handsaw marks—and now, whitewashed, a third life as a sideboard. In the background, an antique bookcase serves double duty as storage for an eclectic collection of ducks—from Grandpa's handmade decoy to various decorative pieces found around the property.

SHAKE IT!

When we "inherited" a random assortment of s&p shakers while rehabbing the resort, we decided to keep going. (My husband made me stop at thirty sets, lest I become a full-fledged pack rat.)

ABOVE AND LEFT Salt and pepper shakers gained popularity in the 1940s with the advent of commercial ceramics, making it easier to manufacture a range of themes and styles. Before you knew it, nearly every roadside pit stop had its own version. And thank heavens; how else would I have a found a Wisconsin-themed girl and boy squirrel set?

CHEERS

Colorful, silk-screened shot glasses have been common since the 1940s. Popular low-cost items from souvenir shops at tourist destinations around the world, they served as reminders of all the places an American family had traveled. Today, vintage ones are cheap and easy to find at garage sales and thrift stores. The simple truth is that doing a round of shots from plain glasses is just boring.

COCKTAIL, ANYONE?

All of our vintage barware came from hand-me-downs and yard sales. Even the bar itself was salvaged from a former employer unloading his furnishings while moving. Moral of the story: patience pays. Martini shakers, bar accessories, and glassware make great displays for two reasons: they're easily accessible and they are instant design when grouped (nearly any combination makes a retro, simple display).

RIGHT Our barware collection makes a great display, though it certainly gets its fair share of mileage.

COCKTAIL HOUR

Retro glass sets and martini shakers like the ones shown are easy to find if you possess at least two of the following:

1 Patience to dig through charity thrift store mountains
2 The time to make the yard sale rounds in old neighborhoods
3 Nerves for competing and bidding at estate auctions

DINING AL FRESCO

Keeping a collection of vintage folding chairs on hand means always being able to make room for unexpected dinner guests. Like the wooden chairs we inherited when we bought the camp, many tell the story of their original owner, in this case the University of Wisconsin, which is stamped on the backrest. When your local churches, VFW halls, and schools upgrade to modern metal folding chairs, they're often happy to unload the old wooden versions for a song.

RIGHT Vintage folding tables placed end to end make for dramatic lakeside dining. A bolt of period-appropriate fabric from a wholesale fabric store gets converted into an inexpensive tablecloth and unifies the otherwise random assortment of folding tables. In the background on the right, an old enamel pot becomes an impromptu wine chiller at the outdoor self-serve bar.

BELOW A vintage miner's lunch pail is repurposed as a utensil caddy, while an old picnic basket lined with a tea towel holds the evening's condiments.

SERVE WARE

I subscribe to the philosophy that one of the best ways to display your vintage serve ware is in use. We put several of our collections in action at once: Fiesta Ware plates, pie stands, and vintage linens. It's all in the display. A lovely or unique dish can make a plate of Twinkies look like a million bucks. Or at least $5.

RIGHT Because most of the doors at our camp had skeleton key locks, we found the keys everywhere. To build your own collection, look at flea markets, where you can expect to pay a buck or two each. (And it's just fun to imagine what types of exotic doors and trunks they may have unlocked.)

OPPOSITE A collection of vintage table napkins get customized with homemade hand tags in a contrasting color and tied with baker's twine.

TOP Milk glass is opaque white glass that was originally manufactured in Venice in the sixteenth century, where it was made to look like porcelain. Recent examples found at most thrift stores for a couple bucks are mass produced and of a lower quality, usually reproductions of popular collectible pieces and patterns. The collection shown here started with several pieces we found in boxes down in the basement.

ABOVE Although souvenir state plates date back to the late 1800s, they became more popular with the advent of modern-day air and auto travel. A proudly displayed collection of state plates was a sign that the owner had the time and means to travel the country. Although many souvenir plates are unmarked, you'll find some with well-known manufacturers, such as Wedgwood, Vernon Kilns, Homer Laughlin, and Salem China Company. We found more of these at a yard sale to build on the original Florida plate shown above.

TEA TIME

Tea cups were a common find around the property: orphans from full tea sets that guests brought from home over the years. The variety of colors and patterns makes for a simple, elegant grouping. Like all of our collections, they aren't just unique display items; they are there to be used. Old teakettles can be found for as low as fifteen bucks. But buyer beware: they don't always smell like an old English blend. . . .

RIGHT Our teakettles found a home perched above the stove (so our English friends can have easy access).

BELOW We also reincarnated an old homemade chicken feeder (that a friend picked up via flea) as another display for one of our coffee cup collections. It keeps them tidy and out of the way, but the real benefit is that it's easy transportation for outdoor impromptu coffee bar setups for al fresco breakfasts.

This fragile collection contrasts well with the hardware-store storage bin they're displayed in.

SHAYNA ON APARTMENT THERAPY POSTED ABOUT HOW SHE FREED AN ANTIQUE KETTLE FROM ODORS

1 Boiled a mixture of white vinegar with water, let it sit and soak.
2 Scrubbed with baking soda and water, let it sit and soak.
3 Repeated. Again and again and again.
4 Wrote to Apartment Therapy for help, got more tips.
5 Scrubbed inside with half of a lemon and salt.
6 Attacked with Bon Ami (probably could have also used Barkeeper's Friend).
7 Scrubbed with ketchup and salt.
8 Repeated everything, then repeated again.
9 Sniff sniff!
10 Boiled water for tea and enjoyed.

—ApartmentTherapy.com

TOOLS AND UTENSILS

ABOVE AND RIGHT No such thing as "for decoration only": every last measuring cup, sifter, and grater earns its keep in our main kitchen (save the meat grinder—I wouldn't know where to start with that thing, so we leave the sausage making to the professionals). Bonus: these tools are the cheapest and easiest items to find in the kitchen bins at thrift stores. You could have a whole collection for less than a ten-dollar investment.

old school charm
Vintage cookie cutters and other kitchen tools work just as well as their modern plastic counterparts, with a thousand times the charm. There's just something more gratifying about baking with lovingly used kitchenware that you know has already brought smiles to countless grandchildren over several generations. We found a holiday assortment in one of the kitchens, and I've not been able to stop compulsively buying them since.

ABOVE When cooking with vintage kitchenware, on vintage stoves, in vintage kitchens, it's nearly sacrilegious to use anything other than vintage cookbooks. This random assortment was discovered in unexpected corners of the camp.

LEFT Fish molds are gross. Sorry, they just are. Nothing good ever came from a fish mold, except the mold itself. When emptied of jelly meat or blood sausage jelly, they are actually quite appealing, especially if you hang them in a cluster. Long live the fish mold.

Vintage wine "tasters" get reincarnated as a wind charm, with only five minutes and a yard of string.

ROLLING OF THE PINS

No vintage kitchen is complete without at least one of these, or in my case, a *ginormous* collection, in each of the four kitchens, no less. . . . (My friend prefers to call this hoarding.) Types of rolling pins:

- **ROD**: thin rods typically made of wood around two to three centimeters in diameter. They're used by rolling the hollow tube, or "rod," across the dough using your palms. The basic wooden rolling pins are the oldest and easiest to find (many being simple tubes of wood).
- **ROLLER**: a thick, heavy roller made of a variety of materials around seven to ten centimeters in diameter with thinner handles that extend through the roller. They are used by grasping the handles and pushing the pin across the dough.

We use old flour tins from the pantry as handy stove-top storage for our vintage kitchen tools. This assortment of green wood-handled utensils found a new home among the green ceramics, jadeite, and serving tray. Displays of utensils work best if you group by hue because of their limited color and material palette. Red options are also easy to find, as design-conscious postwar housewives liked to be able to color coordinate.

CONTAINERS

get it together already Most folks have one junk drawer. I have, well . . . I'm not sure that I can put a number on it. When you're faced with a similar dilemma, vintage swimming pool lockers and other unexpected interesting containers are the best possible solution—more places to hide things (like new collections) from your husband.

ENTERTAINING SCHEDU

WEEK

EARHOLE   8/1

SUMMIT FAMILY RE.   8/8

SHERMAN FAM. RE.   8/15
+ GOLDEN

KIDS CAMP ————— 8/22

ART CAMP ————— 9/5

ALEXEI+MARY WEDDING— 9/26

HALLOWEEN ————— 10/3

ABOVE Displaying collections in a culled-down color palette helps pull together a simple, rustic kitchen.

LEFT A vintage photo we discovered from the 1950s at the restaurant bar.

OPPOSITE A trio of vintage general store candy jars sits atop swimming pool lockers in the main kitchen. What do candy jars have to do with lockers? Absolutely nothing—and that's the beauty of it. A room that's completely decked out in a single theme runs the risk of feeling too "matchy-matchy." It's far more interesting to mix and match for an end-result room that feels less run-of-the-mill.

RETHINKING CONTAINERS

We found a couple of beer bottles and cans left behind from the fifties in a trapdoor under the living room floor, enough to start a collection that we use for display and sometimes as quirky bud vases.

fact

Before pull-tab beer was invented, bottles came with special opening tools that looked like big, old-fashioned door keys, which reminded folks of church doors. These bottle openers, also known as church keys, were commonly branded and given away by beer and soda brewers.

LEFT One of our original valet key boards gets a second life reincarnated as an instant display in the pantry.

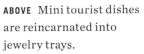

ABOVE Mini tourist dishes are reincarnated into jewelry trays.

ABOVE LEFT There's no such thing as too much of a good thing. Case in point: the five bread boxes I have amassed to line the top of the cupboards in the "mint kitchen" (named for the color of the kitchen and accessories).

LEFT After you buy common grocery store tea bags, toss the modern packaging and store them in vintage tea tins.

WHO WE OWE THE FABULOUS CREDIT OF FOOD PRESERVATION TO

Napoleon, in eighteenth-century France (in an effort to find a way to preserve food for his troops), offered a prize to whoever came up with a solution. Nicolas-François Appert won. He developed a method he likened to wine preservation. His success came from experimentation with heating and sealing jars airtight.

WHY WE CALL THEM BALL JARS

John L. Mason invented them in 1858. A popular manufacturer of them was the "Ball Corp.," thus "Ball jar" was born.

OPPOSITE A simple diner check holder—easy to find in commercial kitchen catalogs—is perfect to casually display a collection of vintage photos in the kitchen. Extra perk: it's easy to rotate your collection and swap out shots. (Side note: Some like to say that buying antique pictures of strangers is a way of collecting "instant ancestors." By that definition alone, I have the largest family tree known to man.)

LEFT A "faux" canning taking place—our friend Christine helps "jar" local honey in mini jelly jars to send out as holiday gifts.

tip

Don't be afraid to let old containers wander out of the kitchen. They make practical and character-laden storage solutions for just about anything, from scrapbooking and desk supplies to sewing kits.

WAYS TO REPURPOSE THE LOWLY BOTTLE

- **GLASS CANNING JARS:** while still quite useful for their originally intended purpose, these also make great storage containers for smaller collections such as marbles, buttons, or seashells. We use several as candleholders. They are commonly known as Mason or Ball jars after the popular manufacturers. While most can be had for just a few bucks, there have been instances of rare items going for as much as an unbelievable thirty thousand dollars. One of my favorite (and quickest) collection displays is a Ball jar crammed to the rim with antique clay marbles.

- **RETIRED MILK BOTTLES:** use them as simple and inexpensive vases. Bottles like these start at four dollars and can be found at any flea market, and sometimes, if you're lucky, en masse at yard sales.

OPPOSITE Milk bottles from my hometown dairy become impromptu bud vases.

fact
S.C. Dyke & Company turned out up to one million clay marbles per day. This mass-production made them cheap and plentiful, and a child could walk with a whole handful of "commies," the nickname for common clay marbles. —hubpages.com

. . . and tartan for all From blankets and overcoats to coolers and jugs, tartan patterns were all the rage beginning in the fifties, a trend started by Queen Victoria when she decorated Balmoral Castle in Scottish tartan. She said that she wished to make tartan desirable throughout the world. Mission accomplished.

HAVE BASKET, WILL TRAVEL

Although vintage picnic baskets, coolers, and jugs can range widely in color scheme and design, they'll hold together nicely as a collection if you vary the pattern. In fact, variety gives the much-needed visual interest that would be lacking in a overly matched display. *Country Living* magazine wrote that "the picnic basket was born in 1901 when British luxury-goods retailers like Asprey started stocking hampers filled with tableware for motorists to enjoy on country drives." We keep them in our trunk. And pantry. And basement. And, well . . . I guess we may have enough already.

For all of you out there asking yourselves what the heck the difference is between plaid and tartan. . . . Technically, *plaid* refers to a traditional Scottish shawllike garment that is worn slung over the shoulder, commonly made of material with a tartan pattern. But to most of us today, *plaid* refers to any tartan pattern. Our collection includes a few we found on the grounds, but most were sourced at my three favorite haunts: the Salvation Army, the Brown Elephant, and the Unique thrift store chains.

LEFT AND OPPOSITE There are no slackers in this house; every vintage jug, picnic basket, and thermos puts in its time for its intended purpose. Shown here are some of the wares we found on the property and augmented with flea market finds.

We found these three cans in the basement, full of nails and steel wool, and after a serious scrubbing, they were reborn into caddies used to run out to the picnic table for last-minute cookouts.

hint

Keep extra cans on hand so you can rotate them into service. The old graphics, fonts, illustrations, and colors bring visual interest and intrigue to even the most modest of kitchens.

ART FROM THE LABELS OF CANNED GOODS

Another term for a vintage vegetable can label is *readymade art.* Honestly, nothing is easier or more instant—I love to stick them on my refrigerators, or inside kitchen cupboard doors for an instant charm facelift. Vegetable-can labels are somewhat rare, and therefore hard to find at the average antique booth at a flea market. So if you're in the market for labels, try searching online first. One great source is thelabelman.com, which carries a large selection as well as some fabulous antique crate labels.

RIGHT At this camp, nothing really gets retired. Case in point, old food containers still serve their originally intended purposes: a Tom Thumbs Soda Cracker tin is used to store snacks, and a vintage galvanized milk delivery box is repurposed as a cooler.

hint

A word of warning: If you truly have what you think to be a very valuable antique, such as a century-old Tiffany lamp, you'd be advised to meet with a professional in person.

what it's worth already

Unless you happen to be in town when the *Antiques Roadshow* visits, most folks won't seek out professional appraisal services for their antiques. The trend of online appraisals has been catching on for its convenience, speed, and affordability. Here are some of my favorite sites:

WHATSITWORTHTOYOU.COM offers a wide range of appraisal services, from cheap entry-level appraisals to deluxe and express services, plus resource directories, courses, and more. This site even offers a "collection appraisal" service, which comes with the era, description, condition, appraiser comments, current fair market value, and replacement costs.

ANTIQUEAPPRAISALS.NET offers a more costly approach, with fees starting at more than $120 per item, which gives you a detailed itemization of the value, how the appraiser reached this conclusion, and all the comparable items similar to your item that have been sold in the past based on information in the site's database. It might not be the ideal site for the "found, free or flea" items, but it's good to have on hand when you find that uberspecial antique in Grandma's attic.

OLDANDSOLD.COM With a fee of ten bucks or so and less than four days' turnaround, this site is hard to beat. And you can even search its past auctions for sold values. This site offers a ton of information for nearly all aspects of collecting.

2

COLLECTED

FROM THE

BEDROOM

sleeping, reading,
chambers of solitude

The first thing that came to mind when we started sifting through the antique linen trunk? Linen sheets that have been line-dried for fifty-plus years have a special, comforting, familiar quality that just can't be replicated with a trip to the bedding department at your local megamall.

There's just something more inviting about objects that were used, and loved, and provided comfort to others before, that give them depth and character. When I came to this realization, I started seeking out well-worn linens in place of the modern versions. And if it was imprinted with the name of a hotel chain from the 1950s or a hand-embroidered kid's name from summer camp—even better. But the day I swapped out my under-the-bed clumsy plastic storage tub for a vintage steamer trunk was the turning point. The replacement trunk I found was a simple, handmade storage box that had at one time contained someone's entire life possessions. Packed to start a new life in a strange country, it had been hand-inscribed a century earlier with the address from Denmark going to "Nort Amerika." Since that day, I've

OPPOSITE The subtle colors of the chair and books are echoed in the vintage clothes hangers, the dried flowers, and the painting.

PREVIOUS PAGES, ABOVE LEFT A stack of pretty vintage linens we keep on hand for guests.

PREVIOUS PAGES, BELOW LEFT Four things these paintings have in common: color scheme, frame color, era, and subject matter. When you have two or more details in common, the likelihood of a cohesive collection is much greater.

PREVIOUS PAGES, RIGHT Who says a bedroom has to be inside? Once we outfitted this hammock, it became the most popular reading nook at the camp.

never been able to pass up a vintage trunk as a replacement for a modern storage box. And yet the most exciting yard-sale find to date was a large carpenter's traveling trunk—I got it home to discover it had a false bottom that was filled with a journeyman's letters dating back to the 1880s. Through reading his letters, I discovered that this man had carried this trunk with him his entire adult life. He had been separated from his family, and the one consistent thing that he had to rely on was this simple wooden box that housed the tools of his trade and the things most important to him—the correspondence that sustained his solitary life on the road as an itinerant carpenter. I keep my collections of linens in trunks like these at the foot of most guest beds. They're always brimming with vintage chenille bedspreads, antique books of poems, and stacks of period postcards . . . meant to re-create for our guests that same sense of discovery.

LEFT Our friend Jane making the rounds to the cabins with a fresh stack of vintage throws.

OPPOSITE Long live the chenille throw. If there is one simple thing you can add to a room to inject nostalgia, this is it.

NOT JUST FOR TAILGATING

The retro fifties boy's-room curtains that we found in the linen closet inspired one of the bedrooms. Its old-school sports pattern became the theme of a room that we filled with skis, rackets, baseball gear, and books . . . proof that sometimes a single object can inspire a collection that you can build an entire room around.

ABOVE My favorite detail in this sporty bedroom: an original 1940s-era Boy Scout troop leader hat (found at an antiques store). Admittedly, it wasn't found, free, or flea—I broke my own rule, but it was 50 percent off, and that counts!

RIGHT This old trunk is one of the dozens around the property that holds the extra linens needed to accommodate folks coping with the weather as the seasons change in Wisconsin.

FORM + FUNCTION FOR SIMPLE DISPLAYS

When designing interiors with collections, I like to start with a basic need—like storage or seating—then find a novel way to use my collections to address the need. When it comes to color, there are no hard-and-fast rules, but you can't go wrong with restraint. Let the subtle colors of a few objects echo the hues in surrounding pieces. A restrained color palette will also unify an otherwise random assortment of items, from an antique, handmade travel trunk, to vintage folding chairs, to a classroom world map, to an electric fan.

LEFT Camp stools, all in a row. Another example of simple camp style, and for a very little investment (at less than ten dollars each).

simple. elegant. easy.

The smallest common details can hold a collection together. In the tableau on the opposite page, the red in the book spines complements the thermos.

TIMEPIECES AS ART

I can't understand why anyone would have wanted to use an alarm clock while on vacation, but we found no shortage of them at Wandawega. Starting your own collection is easy—there's an abundance of very cheap models. The obsessed should check out discoverclocks.com.

FOR DISPLAY ONLY

Displaying plates or paintings on a wall is one of the oldest and most common ways to decorate with a collection. A few ideas to make it happen:

HANGING TIP Arrange the collection on newspaper in the composition you like and trace around the pieces. Then hang up the newspaper (as a sort of template) to keep from making a million unnecessary holes. (I learned the hard way.)

HAND-PAINTED TRAYS Picked up at a church charity shop, these were converted into wall art. I simply used inexpensive wire plate hangers from the dollar store.

PAINT-BY-NUMBER POOCHES

In the 1950s, when the paint-by-number kit was invented, retailers welcomed them as a "transition item," estimating that a good percentage of paint-by-number hobbyists would go on to purchase traditional art supplies to create their own artwork. It swept the nation as a popular pasttime, and the kits are now easy to find and becoming more collectible.

OIL PAINTINGS

These don't need to be expensive. If you keep your eye out at thrift stores and yard sales (like we did), it's easy to find truckloads of them, executed by amateur painters. There is a certain charm in the naïve quality of this type of painting, and when grouped together, they can take on an entirely new look.

"Although many critics saw 'number painting' as a symbol of the mindless conformity gripping 1950s America, paint by number had a peculiarly American virtue. It invited people who had never before held a paintbrush to enter a world of art and creativity." —"Paint by Number," Smithsonian National Museum of American History website

HOUSES OF THE
BIRD VARIETY

Folks have been making birdhouses dating back to early Native American tribes who hung hollow gourds to attract purple martins. Today, gardeners love them to attract birds for pest control, and bird-watchers like creating havens that make it easier for them to enjoy their hobby.

At our old lakefront retreat, tons of these things have accumulated over the years, courtesy of camp projects, thoughtful handymen accustomed to using every piece of scrap wood, and birders looking to make the most of their time in the country. When these old wooden shelters are too far gone to protect their former inhabitants from the weather, we made sure to give them a second life as decorative items in the bedroom as a way to "bring the outside in." After all, who says birdhouses only belong in the trees?

Because of its twenty-five acres of trees, Camp Wandawega has always been a popular bird retreat. So it's no surprise that we occasionally continue to find handmade birdhouses nestled in the branches. Eventually, they drop from their perches, and we're waiting to catch them, to retire them to a bench or shelf—or even better, to the bedroom.

RIGHT AND OPPOSITE Shown here are examples of my favorites birdhouses in action around the campgrounds.

get immersed. then get busy.

BE INSPIRED Some of the most beautiful and simple solutions are found walking down Michigan Avenue. The Ralph Lauren store chain has gorgeous window displays for lodge inspiration, Abercrombie and Fitch has nailed the Nantucket-camp style, and Anthropologie is renowned for its for unique ways to display objects, art, anything. But nothing beats boutiques districts. From Bleecker Street in Greenwich Village to Notting Hill in London, every major city has at least one district of tiny shops bursting with amazingly talented people who know how to put it together. Don't be afraid to take pictures (just always ask permission first!). Shopkeepers are typically friendly and accommodating if you're honest enough to admit that you covet their style. There's a lot to be learned from photo stylists—a good one can make a stack of paperclips and a roll of duct tape look like artwork.

BUILD A SCRAPBOOK Stop throwing away the catalogs and magazines. Keep those Restoration Hardware and Pottery Barn mailings and don't toss the old issues of *Country Living* and *Martha Stewart Living*. If you see something you like, tear it out and paste it up on your bulletin board or scrapbook wall. Even if you don't have time to start the project today, you will. And when that time comes, you'll be glad you saved the image.

Then, when you are ready to tackle that stack of plates to arrange, don't copy the photo, just use it as your launch pad. A little confidence and a lot of trial and error will take you a long way. Look for inspiration in unlikely places. . . . I love to collect vintage decorating magazines and books, for instance. I typically find enough inspiration from one 1960s-era *Better Homes and Gardens* to fill a binder.

GET THE REAL DEAL I still find that the best inspiration for camp, cabin, cottage, and country style is to go straight to the source. Visit old Boy and Girl Scout camps. Drive to the Adirondacks and tour old lodges and cabins that have been preserved and converted into museums. Don't be afraid to go to "re-creation" educational exhibits that showcase pioneer-style shelters. (There is a great one called "Old World Wisconsin" that we visit yearly just to be reminded of how to strip down a room if I feel the hoarding urge coming on.) Instead of buying a knock-off new sign with modern silk-screen printing that says "Welcome to Camp," make your own with vintage wood scrap—or better yet, if you find one from a real abandoned camp, get it by any means necessary (legally, of course).

VACANCY

CABIN
3

TO THE PIER

WANDAWEGA
LAKE RESORT

PLEASE
Help keep this place clean
State Board of Health

ROOM
For Rent

ENTRANCE

CAMP SHOWER

HILLTOP CAMPGROUND

TENTS ONLY

18

KEEP OFF THE GRASS

EXIT →

MECHANICAL ROOM

CHAPEL

CABIN 1

3

COLLECTED

FROM THE

GREAT
OUTDOORS

fishing, boating,
playing with abandon

When I cracked open the attic door and found the old tennis racket hanging from the chimney stack, it looked remarkably familiar. It wasn't particularly unique—it was just like any racket you'd find at your thrift store. But its home was this summer camp . . . and it was a reminder that when you strip away all of our modern-day trappings, we inevitably find ourselves enjoying the same things our grandparents did.

This nostalgia is heightened when you embrace sports with the same equipment of our ancestors. The grip of a hundred-year-old Louisville Slugger just feels different from its modern-day aluminum equivalent. And your grandfather's tennis score is far more impressive when you actually try to hit a game using what he had to use: an old leather-wrapped wooden version (like the ones we found). Something about our summer camp beckoned us to embrace sports old-school style, and our friends seemed to prefer the weathered and worn versions of the sporting equipment we inherited with the camp. This hunch would be confirmed when, on one sunny afternoon, I set out two croquet sets on the lawn—one with handles so worn you could barely read the maker, and the other, a brand new, freshly painted "Made In

OPPOSITE, ABOVE We found minnow buckets scattered all over the property, dating from the twenties to the sixties. These days, their primary use is for toad catching at our annual summer kids camp weekend.

OPPOSITE, BELOW One of my favorite finds was an attic trunk stashed full of vintage wooden tennis rackets (which I promptly hosed off, as it looked like six generations of mice had built a condo in there).

Taiwan" version—everyone chose the former. And so it began. Archery, snowshoeing, tennis, canoeing, potato sack races, tug-o-war, skating, skiing, and sledding all became more of a challenge—and more rewarding—using the vintage gear.

As always, all of the collections started with a single object found at the camp—until the collections grew so large we had to convert one of the camp bedrooms to a "sports equipment room" just to house the finds. The tennis racket from the attic would become the centerpiece on a wall installation, surrounded by others like it . . . but it's a functional display as well. When guests want to practice their backhand, we send them straight to the wall to grab a racket.

LEFT My husband, David, forty years ago, wearing his favorite little orange life vest that we later uncovered in a storage trunk and now have on display on a door. It inspired the rest of the collection we've built of similar vintage jackets.

treasure in the attic. and basement. and trunks . . . The previous camp owners left a collection of vintage rowboats, oars, and other paraphernalia that we now enjoy. We unearthed stacks and stacks of life jackets, piles of minnow buckets, and boxes of lures galore. . . . This place was a virtual treasure trove of summers past. Everything we discovered was either incorporated into the interior decor or used to stock the sports equipment room for guest use.

THE ART OF THE OAR, IN FIVE WAYS

1 Wall hanging (strung up with fishing line)
2 Coat rack (with nail heads inserted as "hooks")
3 A welcome sign for an entrance
4 A crisscrossed installation on a cabin facade
5 In use (they still haven't invented a better way to move a canoe)

ABOVE AND RIGHT Our oar collection is so extensive that we have plenty of extras to use as decor around the camp. The "sports equipment hall" on the property sees a lot of action—we used bicycle-hanging hooks from the Container Store to keep the canoe paddles separate from the rowboat oars. We call one of our bedrooms, where we've anchored a couple of oars to the wall, the "oar room."

We love to actually use our vintage water skis, but when they aren't being used, we hang them in a crisscross on the wall of a cabin. They have some serious old-school charm.

THE ONE THAT GOT AWAY

Finding worthwhile bargains is like fishing: the more often you cast, the more likely you are to reel in a great catch. Like a good fisherman, get to know your waters. Know when local thrift stores restock. Watch the papers for estate and big yard sales. Get on the mailing lists for church, charity, and thrift store sales. And check your favorite keyword searches at online auctions and classifieds at least weekly.

FOR THE LOVE OF FISH

We found many, many minnow buckets all over the campground. The design and the graphics of these vessels have changed very little in the past five decades, which is why I find them so charming.

RIGHT A glimpse of the enormous collection of minnow buckets we have (now found out in nearly every corner) at Camp Wandawega.

OPPOSITE Here, fishy fishy . . . Mounted fish are almost a mandate for any camp- or cabin-themed decor. We were lucky to have found a few of them at our retreat, but happy to have an excuse to go shopping to build on the collection. Some of these guys have seen better days, but you don't notice the missing scales if you stand back to take in the installation as a whole.

A simple vignette like this can be constructed and placed inside a cabin room for an instant *River Runs Through It* vibe. (And it doesn't need to break the bank . . . all you need are a few fishing-themed items.)

tip
Hold a fly fishing lure
over boiling water if it
gets crushed or mis-
shapen. The steam
should help it snap
back into shape.

ABOVE An effortless way to display a life-ring collection indoors (when you no longer have a use for them outside): Hang them on window hardware overlooking a scenic area (in this case, the sun porch on the lodge overlooking the lake). It helps to have oversight; in this case it was our dog, Frankie.

LEFT Two of the original property owners on Lake Wandawega—taken by each other—back in the 1950s.

OPPOSITE The theme of sports and games is carried throughout the sun porch—on the walls and in the bookcase.

"Trees are your best antiques."
—Alexander Smith (1830–1867)

LONG LIVE THE POTATO SACK

Repurpose the fabric of a potato sack to upholster furniture, make pillows, or even craft into bags. Online, you can find vintage potato sacks ranging from ten to thirty bucks, depending on the age, condition, and brand.

OPPOSITE I discovered these potato sacks at a barn sale.

RIGHT Croquet has long been a favorite summer pastime, and we found evidence of this one afternoon in the attic rafters of the main lodge. Tucked away in a trunk was a stack of old mallets and balls, not a complete set— but enough to keep ourselves entertained. It is one of my favorite finds from the attic. Even if you don't have enough equipment for a serious game, they make for a cute display in a vertical basket (like the antique apple-rolling type shown here).

WHEN LOOKING FOR RACE-WORTHY POTATO SACKS, KEEP THESE TIPS IN MIND

1 Turn them inside out to evict all the bugs that have been camping out (or are probably dead) in there.
2 A little Febreze and an old-fashioned line-drying will help fresh them up.
3 Know that with kids climbing in and out of them, they'll likely tear eventually. Burlap gets brittle with age, and we've noticed that mold quickly forms if the bag is left in a damp place, which also weakens the fibers.

RIGHT The three most popular games at picnics: potato sack race, tug-o-war, and the three-legged race.

WHAT BASEBALLS ARE MADE OF
(STARTING FROM THE INSIDE OUT)

ABOVE Some collections are an automatic display depending on how you store them. Something simple like this wire basket (most likely a former egg basket) is perfect for our baseball collection.

Cork. Rubber. More rubber. Gray wool winding. More wool. Cotton finish winding. Cowhide leather. Waxed cotton thread stitching.

One way to collect baseballs: ballhawking (catching home-run balls outside of Wrigley Field in Chicago). According to Mike Diedrich (producer and director of the movie *Ballhawks*), one expert, Moe, has amassed a collection of more than 4,500 baseballs over the past forty years, which is valued at more than $300,000.

A SUMMER CAMP JUST ISN'T CAMP WITHOUT ARCHERY.

The places to have the most luck sourcing vintage archery gear? EBay, Etsy, Craigslist, but, above all, flea markets are the most fun. We sourced many of our collections from several different sets and display them hanging in their archery pack when not in use.

"Even with no money, everyone could collect something." —OTTO C. LIGHTNER, avid collector and publisher of the magazine *Hobbies,* one of the first antiques and collectibles publications

HAVING A GREAT TIME, WISH YOU WERE HERE

They're so cheap, they're almost free. You can find vintage postcards virtually anywhere, and in a grouping, they add instant character and texture to any room. The ones on display here are tacked up to the frame of a vintage Boy Scout tent on the "tent hill" overlooking the lake. Notice the center "Wisconsin" card—it's a repro from a vintage card we found at an antiques store.

BADGE OF HONOR

Nothing says summer camp like the Boy Scouts of America patches. There are scores of websites dedicated to collecting BSA and GSA memorabilia, if you'd like to fashion a jacket like the one we keep at our camp (donated by a friend).

OPPOSITE When we erected a collection of vintage Boy Scout tents at the camp, it proved to be the ideal place to display my stockpile of BSA gear and collectibles.

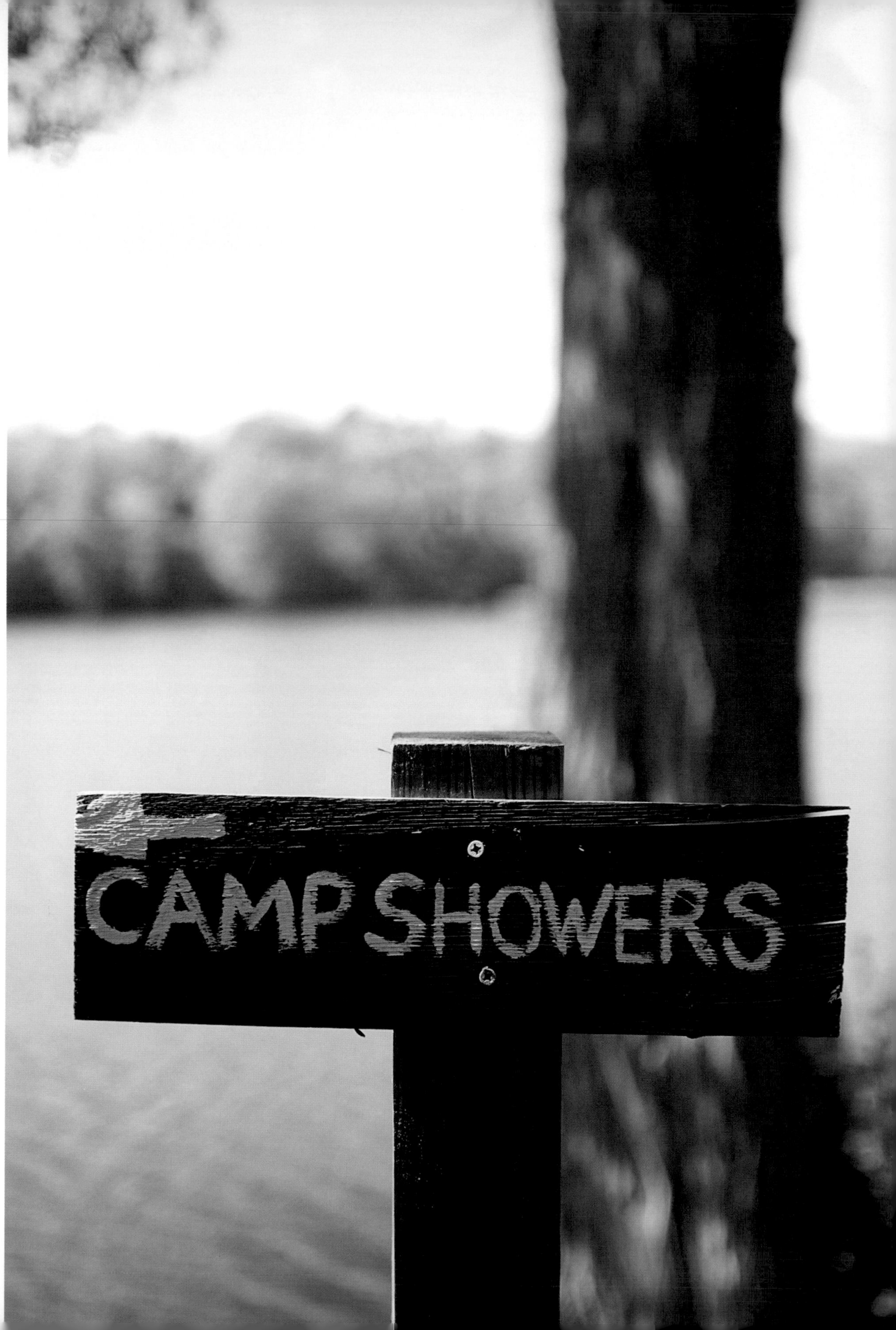
CAMP SHOWERS

SPIGOT HANDLES REINCARNATED INTO TOWEL HOOKS

STEP 1: Look for spigot handles of similar sizes, in a variety of colors.

STEP 2: Drill pilot holes into the wall. Use wall anchors in drywall or plaster.

STEP 3: Insert a screw into the handle. "Sleeve" the screw with a common hardware store spring to act as a spacer.

STEP 4: Screw into the desired length, securing the back side with a bolt and washers.

STEP 5: Hang and enjoy!

The *Boy Scout Handbook* says, "A flashlight will be standard issue and should always be packed for easy access, and kept at the ready at all times."

MUMBLETY-PEG

This was an old outdoor game played by kids using pocketknives. I've been told that it was a popular schoolyard game in the nineteenth and first half of the twentieth centuries, but with warranted increased concern over safety, it's no longer mainstream. It did continue as a common summer camp activity, however, up into the 1970s. The general rule as I understand it is that it's played between two people with a pocketknife. In one version, two opponents stand opposite one another with their feet shoulder-width apart. The first player then takes the knife and throws it to "stick" in the ground as close to his own foot as possible. The second player then repeats the process. Whichever player sticks the knife closest to his own foot wins the game. I think a more fitting name for this game might be Insanity, but that's just me.

ABOVE Just part of the collection of the knives found at the camp. The handles of bone, wood, and Bakelite (with inlaid engraved plates) make for a great textural display.

PACK IT UP

When it comes to vintage luggage, I have an obsession bordering on unhealthy. Whenever I visit another country, I'll find an antique trunk or large suitcase, fill it with thrift and junk store treasures, and check it at the airport to ship home. Because of this, I've somehow accumulated an embarrassing amount, which we use as under-bed storage, stacked end tables, and sometimes even for travel. It all started with a handful we found on the campground, left behind by former visitors (those few are still my favorites).

PLATE COLLECTING

Collectible old license plates are sought for their age, color, origin, shape, condition, or the history that goes along with them. Car swap meets, junkyards, dumps, and auto scrap yards are great sources for old license plates. Most collectors choose to seek out ones based on a specific location or a certain year. A general rule of thumb: The older it is, the more dollars it brings. (But truth be told, it's really just about the visual impact of the grouping, regardless of each piece's price tag.)

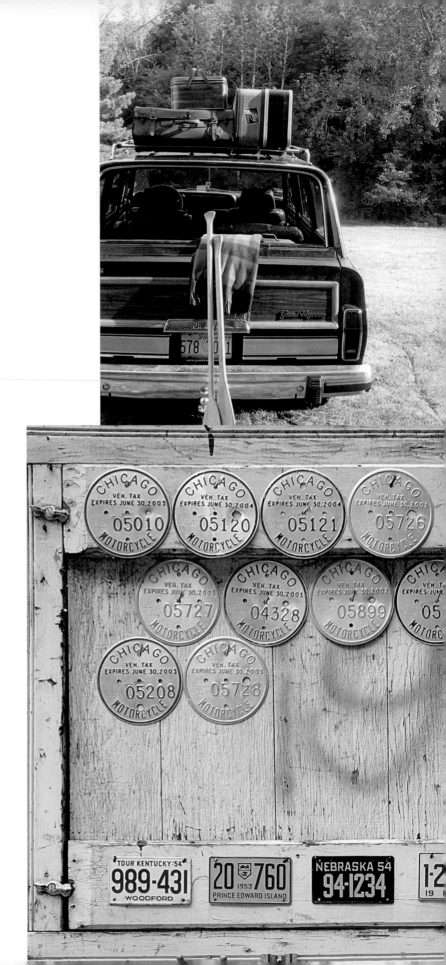

HELMETS: NOT JUST TO PROTECT YOUR NOGGIN ANYMORE

An unexpected storage solution for retired motorcycle helmets: displaying them on the garage door for easy access and a colorful arrangement. The most popular vintage motorcycle helmets to collect are the ones with the metallic "flake" paint job (red and silver, as shown above, are common but they bring the most money). But buyer beware: They may look great lined up on your garage, but ones that date back forty-plus years are likely no longer safe. When it comes to protecting your head, best to invest more than fifteen dollars.

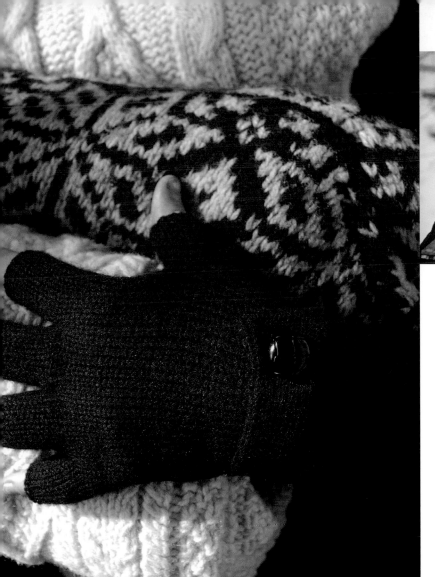

cold hands, warm heart

Although Camp Wandawega was built as a summer resort, it's a surprisingly fun winter retreat as well—and a reason to collect sporting goods for the cold season. (One can never have too many Hudson Bay blankets).

FALL ENTERTAINING IS CHEAP, CHARMING, AND EASY WITH THESE TIPS. . . .

- We always keep a stack of thrift store sweaters on hand to help guests fight off the night-time chill.
- Vintage Boy Scout mugs are durable and practical—each with a unique story to tell.
- In addition to the old sweaters, we also stocked up on stadium blankets. Our collection started with a few we discovered in various rooms, under beds and in trunks.

HOSTESS WITH THE MOSTESS (WOOL CAMP BLANKETS)

We use them all over the camp, from throws on guest beds to a bit of extra padding on the Adirondack chairs on the piers, to a welcome sign waiting with the promise of warmth on the hammocks. If you're patient, you can find them occasionally at resale shops and thrift stores (where you'll get the best prices), but flea markets will typically have them in spades—as will of course eBay (but that, of course, would be cheating the "found, free, or flea" rule).

ABOVE RIGHT I've yet to be turned down when offering up a vintage plaid wood blanket on a cold day. This collection started with one lap blanket we found at the camp, and was augmented from thrift store excursions.

RIGHT In this old photograph, one of the resort visitors on the grounds tests out a pair of skis.

ABOVE AND LEFT A friend of ours from CS Interiors once said that we "have enough plaid to outfit an entire Scottish army in kilts." Some of my favorite ways to work vintage wool throws into a room is to display one simply folded at the end of a bed or stack a half-dozen on a chair for easy access.

PREPARED FOR ANYTHING

The easiest solution ever for guest umbrella storage: Use anything tall—it could be a vertical vintage shipping crate or an antique barrel.

LEFT AND BELOW The more things that you can provide for your guests, the more comfortable their stay will be (and the harder it will be to get them to leave). Case in point: umbrellas, raincoats, and rain boots. Keeping them on hand lined up on a staircase or hanging in a row at a cabin entrance is a welcome sign on a cold, rainy Sunday.

THE LANTERN TREE

Given the number of hurricane lanterns we found strewn about, I can't imagine there having ever been a shortage of them at the camp. Our collection is a combination of new and old, and in a primary color palette, which makes for a great display hanging from tree limbs by our old-school tennis court.

The Standard Novelty Works
of Duncannon, Pennsylvania,
made the famous Lightning
Guider sleds from 1904 to 1990.
—sledworks.com

SNOW SKIS GET A SECOND LIFE

Yes, they're great wall hangers crisscrossed above a mantel, but there's nothing like cross-country skiing with an old pair of hickory skis.

the origins of the shotski

Shotski-ism came from Austria (called *Schnappski*). Traditional alpine shotskis do not have jigger or "schnapp" glasses permanently attached, like the American versions. Instead you simply place the glasses on a ski or in small grooves made for the glasses. Bottoms up!

TRANSLATIONS FOR MITTEN

Danish: *vante*
Dutch: *handschoen*
Finnish: *hansikas*
French: *moufle*
Norwegian: *hanske*
Portuguese: *luva*
Swedish: *vante*

RIGHT Collections are far more attractive when you can actually use them. A basket full of vintage scarves and mittens is a warm welcome sign on a frigid day.

LIGHT 'EM UP

I keep a modest little collection of pipes in an old cigar box. They come in handy when we're outfitting snowmen. Also pictured here is our good boy Frankie (not shown: the biscuit he is sitting still for).

LEFT Antique matchboxes have beautiful labels. Shown here are a few examples from a collection I've been building for years.

EVERY CAMP NEEDS A PENDLETON COLLECTION

Nothing says camp/ cabin/country like the old-school plaid Pendleton shirts. They are still relatively easy to find in vintage clothing stores and online (but you'll pay a premium if you go that route). The best bet for the best prices is to look in thrift stores in popular hunting and fishing locales (think Washington, Vermont, Wisconsin). Many of the seniors in these types of areas were once sportsmen, and they typically retire their gear by donating to local charities. Or you can scoop up an entire collection at once by hitting a yard sale at the right time.

in all fifty states

There is certainly no shortage of great flea markets across the country for us to get our flea fix (thank all things holy). Here are a few great online sources that provide listings by state: greatfleamarket.com, keysfleamarket .com, fleamarketworld.net.

And when you find the one flea market your heart's set on, here are a couple of tips for the trip:

• Shop alone and pick a spot to meet your flea market companions at a later time. If you're on a mission for a particular item, a group will slow you down, as everyone will be seeking out different things. It's easiest to synchronize your watches and regroup at a designated spot at scheduled intervals (or when the truck is full).

• Use the map. Most large fleas provide a booth or row map to help you navigate. Some sort of navigation will not only help you track where you've been but also provide a great way to mark a booth you need to go back to in order to retrieve a large item you paid for but didn't want to haul around all day.

• If you want to avoid the crowds, go the night before (some fleas offer "early shopper" days for an extra fee).

• Leave the extra layers at home, including the purse and bulky wallet (as uncool as belly bags are, nothing ruins the day faster than a pickpocket). Embrace the murse (aka man purse/over-the-shoulder bag).

• Leave the Rolex at home, even if it's a fauxlex. You won't be very effective in your haggling if the vendor thinks that you're loaded. You don't need to dress like a homeless person, but it does help if you're a bit more humble.

• Bring a rolling cart or something else to keep your back in check and to enable you to buy more stuff. Mark my words, you won't regret it.

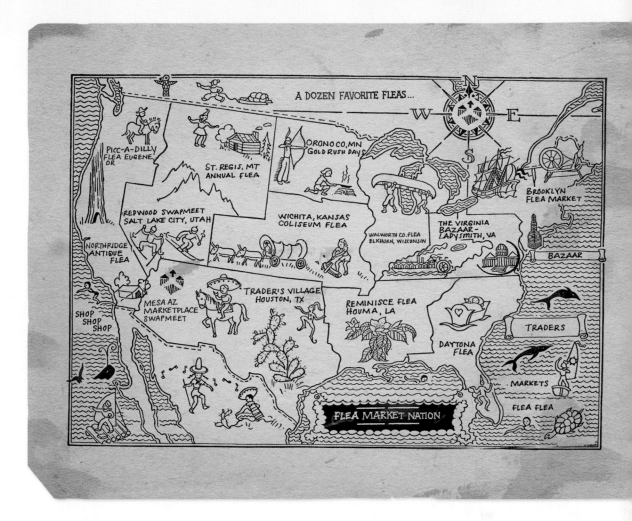

- Look for the bargain table. The dollar tables rock. Don't pass them by; a good chunk of our camp's collections were gleaned from the five-dollar bin that most don't bother to dig through.
- Don't be afraid to negotiate. Vendors expect you to try to talk them down. I usually start with 10 percent at a minimum. It's always worth it (and the more you do it, the easier it gets). If you find someone who won't negotiate, ask them if they would throw in some small extra item instead. And use cash: although some sellers may accept personal checks, or on occasion, credit, you'll find that cash is still king, especially for haggling.
- Bring a tape measure and notes on the room dimensions that you are buying for. Your mother was right—measure twice, buy once (or in my case, measure three times and write it in Sharpie on your hand).

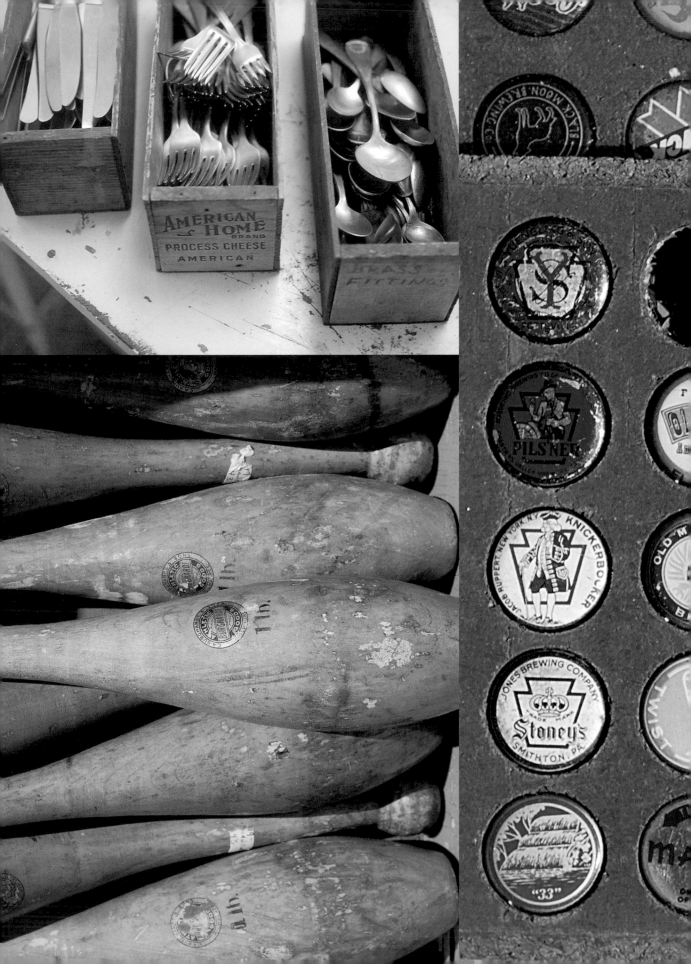

playing, socializing, entertaining

The trophy buried in the bottom of the trunk was inscribed: "First place fishing derby—1945 James Webb." This was most likely one of James's proudest moments. And yet, it was somehow forgotten and discarded, for us to find sixty years later.

It was such a charming reminder of happier times that had taken place there. But it didn't seem right to be left solitary—it begged to be grouped with other trophies, plaques, and engraved cups. With a lot of time and patience, we began gathering other similar pieces, and when we had amassed enough, they became a quaint grouping on a mirrored dresser. A collection of trophies from hard-fought contests, tournaments, and events long forgotten. But it wasn't just trophies that took us back—other smaller items did as well: A simple Fire King bowl placed on a coffee table, filled to the top with dozens of vintage matchbooks, can take you back. Who was it that visited all these amazing places and collected matchbooks as keepsakes? How exactly did Grison's Chicken House at the corner of Van Ness and Pacific in San Francisco "Glorify The American Chicken"? We would never have those answers, but we could group our matchbook finds and display them in a way that lets others sift through and imagine.

The "indoor" collections we found and amassed at the camp have been known to be called knickknacks, curios, tchotchkes, even dust collectors. And we certainly found no shortage of them while cleaning up the place. The one thing each of them had in common was that they each managed to find their way here over the course of the last century. We reasoned that since they had survived this long, we would embrace them and try to find their lost siblings.

OPPOSITE By combining paintings and drawings with three-dimensional objects, we get more visual interest and diversity on our game room wall. The result is an installation that makes the whole wall a single piece of artwork.

old school tunes

Radios were once important sources of entertainment, typically put in a place of prominence. Then, at some point a smaller, shinier version became available and these were tossed in the attic to be forgotten. We embrace them for what they are: simply beautiful objects.

RIGHT Patrons at the bar at Wandawega in the 1940s, the same era as some of the radios we found in the attic.

MUSIC COLLECTIONS

Sheet music is commonly found in a "lot" (a large collection being sold as a set). Musicians typically collect sheet music for a lifetime, so the graphics can vary across several decades—a virtual treasure trove of design. (And it's fun to keep them in the piano bench for guests to pull out randomly and play at dinner parties.)

THREE THINGS YOU MIGHT NOT KNOW ABOUT SHEET MUSIC

1 Vintage sheet music is both beautiful and cheap—it's not uncommon at yard sales to find a crate of vintage sheet music (like the ones shown here), which can be had for a fistful of dollars.
2 The Library of Congress sheet collections includes more than 5.5 million pieces.
3 The generic word for sheet music is *score*, which can also refer to music written for a play, TV, or film.

LUCKY DAY

In one drawer in the parlor, we found a cigar box chock full of poker chips, playing cards, and more vintage dice than we knew what to do with.

CARDS, ANYONE?

One pastime has remained consistent at Camp Wandawega through the past eighty years—card games. So it came as no surprise to find at least one deck in every other room throughout the camp. We started stockpiling and have enough to last several lifetimes.

betcha didn't know . . .

In the twelfth century, the Chinese replaced their bone or ivory playing cards (also called tiles) with a heavy paper kind of playing card.

SOME NUGGETS ABOUT DICE

- "Astragalomancy" is the practice of divination that uses dice. Even today, experienced elbow shakers often call dice "bones" or "devil's bones."

- Dice predate the written word and can be found in almost every culture in the world. Excavations in Egypt have turned up stone dice dating from 2000 BC that look remarkably similar to the modern thing. For his dice, ancient man used, among other things, plum and peach pits, stones, seeds, bones, horn, pottery, pebbles, shells, and, for the most random material source I've ever heard, even *beaver teeth.*

- "Make no bones about it" means nothing has been left to chance. The "bones" of the expression refer to gambling dice.

—bigsiteofamazingfacts.com

"The art of
collecting
beer coasters
even has its
own name:
"tegestology.""
—*Collector's Weekly*

whiskey anyone? Decanters are some of the easiest things to find at thrift stores—and typically for only a few bucks each. They make a great display grouped, a welcome invitation for guests to help themselves.

Heirloom (noun): "A personal possession that usually has a sentimental value which exceeds its monetary value."
—trueblueauctions.com

history
The first matches available for sale appeared
in 1827. It took until the late 1800s for
advertisers to get the idea of putting their
messages on matchbooks. —about.com

OF MATCHES AND BOOKS

Let's face it. Smoking was in vogue in the camp's heyday. Back then, matchboxes and books were custom printed and handed out by nearly every business, everywhere. Accessible and free, they were fun to collect (like the matchbook cover album pictured here), and today, are a small reminder of a simpler time.

ODE TO THE MATCH-MAKERS
Early matches were made manually, and a diligent worker could produce about five thousand matchsticks per hour.

phillumenist (noun)
PRONUNCIATION: \fi-'lü-mə-nist\
ETYMOLOGY: *phil-* + Latin *lumen* light
DEFINITION: one who collects matchbooks or matchbox labels
—*Merriam-Webster's Dictionary*

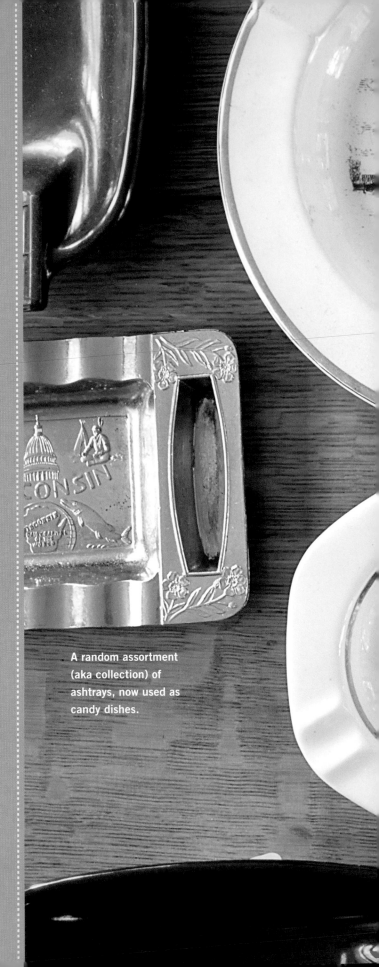

TYPES OF TROPHIES TO COLLECT

- **A LOVING-CUP TROPHY:** a cup shape, usually on a pedestal, with two or more handles, and often made from silver or silver plate
- **HUNTING TROPHIES:** an animal's head mounted to be hung on a wall
- **RESIN TROPHIES:** a trophy that's found in a variety of sports or generic forms (often used for participation awards and custom-made for specific events)

MEMORIES ETCHED IN METAL

Like many of the things we've found at Wandawega since we started our renovation, the trophies carry a history, story, or memory of a proud moment in someone's life. The ones we discovered were typically smaller ribbons or pendants for participation, but they sparked an interest in building a more elaborate collection, some of which are displayed here on a dresser top in the lodge.

A random assortment (aka collection) of ashtrays, now used as candy dishes.

CITY TOLL BRIDGE
ILLINOIS RIVER
BEARDSTOWN, ILL.

SAVOY HO
FIRENZ

GEORGE DIAMOND

CHARCOAL

BROILED

STEAKS

PALM SPRINGS, CALIFORNIA

CHICAGO - ANT

SOUVENIR OF
TTYSBURG, PA.

NOILLY DRY

NOILLY ROUGE

a fine line On any given Saturday, after I return from a successful flea/thrift/yard sale excursion, I will be called at least one of these names by my husband:

PACK RAT a person who engages in compulsive hoarding (in reference to the pack rat, a bushy-tailed rodent of the genus *Neotoma* of western North America that hoards food and other objects)

MAGPIE someone who collects things that have been discarded by others

HOARDER a person who excessively acquires possessions (and fails to use or discard them). One suggested treatment for hoarding: Find new hobbies.

CREATING VIGNETTES

Think of a theme to unify a group of objects—in this case a misfit family of taxidermy castoffs. We found one of these guys at camp, and adopted the others from Walworth County flea market. We discovered fantastic bear heads and random exotic fish at other fleas, but stuck with the local Wisconsin theme to keep the collection regional. We keep our extended family on display: duck, squirrel, turtle, raccoon, deer, and pheasant. Now if we could only find a chipmunk . . .

LEFT When we found this antique photo of the lodge from the 1920s, I started shopping to re-create the taxidermy vignette on the mantel.

CERAMIC DOGS

My grandmother had a collection large enough to fill several bookshelves. They're very accessible and typically inexpensive. If you can restrain yourself enough to set out only three to five pooches, it makes for a quaint little accent on a side table.

LEFT I'm on a never-ending hunt for vintage magazines to stock each guestroom nightstand.

THE RIGHT WAY TO USE A HURRICANE LANTERN

Follow these quick instructions on how not to burn down your cabin while trying to operate a lantern.

1 **HOW MANY PEOPLE DOES IT TAKE TO . . .** (One, if you read closely.) Unscrew the detachable piece from the hurricane lamp so you can fill it three-quarters of the way up with oil.

2 **FEEDING THE FIRE:** Prefeed the wick through the insert on the detachable piece from the bottom through the top while using the turning wheel to bring it through. (Make sure the wick clears all metal parts by ¼ inch.)

3 **HOW NOT TO LOSE YOUR EYEBROWS:** As you're feeding the wick into the base, reattach the metal piece on the slotted wick holder to the metal piece affixed to the base. Skin-saving tip: Clean up any spilled oil before getting anywhere near a flame.

4 **LET THERE BE LIGHT.** Light that wick, already! Then replace the glass globe to fit over the base and spin the knob to adjust your flame size.

Note: I don't want to be responsible for a house fire, so be sure to follow directions from more official sources!

ON DISPLAY When in doubt, always try the simple technique of displaying similar objects to make an interesting composition. In this case, a grouping of camp-inspired objects and artwork. Or, more obviously, the collection of lanterns on the ledge.

TREETOP HOUSE

Our friends built us "Tom's Treehouse" (named after my dad) solely from salvaged materials. It proudly sits in the center of the camp and features an antler chandelier made up of sheds that we found on our hiking trails and gifts from hometown friends. For this fixture, we replaced the chains with rope for a rustic end result.

ANTLERS GET A SECOND CHANCE

My brother made us another antler chandelier as a wedding gift, comprising sheds he found as well as antlers from trophy deer of other friends and family members. Also shown here on the mantel is the old entrance sign; you'll notice that the *W*'s have been replaced with *V*'s, (reflecting the days of the Latvian ownership).

ANTLER CHANDELIER IN THE MAKING

We have several antler chandeliers at the camp. Making your own is remarkably simple (for a small fixture). All you need is a basket of antlers (to be found in nature or at flea markets en masse) and a basic metal u-hook ceiling light fixture (and a teeny bit of patience). Just weave the individual antlers in and through the existing metal brackets of the chandelier until they create tension and can hold themselves in place. (If you need additional security, fishing wire and a hot glue gun works wonders.) Disclaimer: there are lots of professional antler chandelier builders out there who will argue that my method is flimsy and ridiculous, but it's worked for us for the past six years, so I remain optimistic that it's not going to come crashing down on our heads any day soon (fingers crossed).

Tom's Treehouse features panoramic views of the campground.

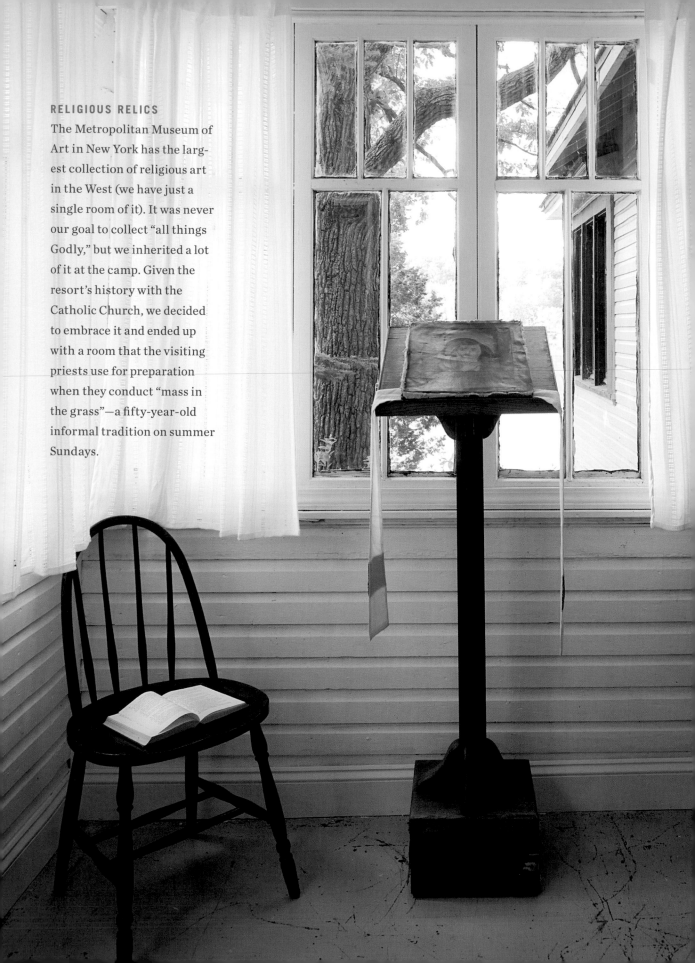

RELIGIOUS RELICS

The Metropolitan Museum of Art in New York has the largest collection of religious art in the West (we have just a single room of it). It was never our goal to collect "all things Godly," but we inherited a lot of it at the camp. Given the resort's history with the Catholic Church, we decided to embrace it and ended up with a room that the visiting priests use for preparation when they conduct "mass in the grass"—a fifty-year-old informal tradition on summer Sundays.

CROSSES, CANDLESTICKS, AND CHRISTIAN ANTIQUES

Because of Camp Wandawega's history of being a Latvian Catholic retreat, it wasn't at all unusual to find so many crucifixes in every possible corner of the property. Every time we found one, we'd add it to the collection in what became known as the chapel. Needless to say, the chapel eventually became so full, we had to find a solution to display the crucifixes. Shown below is one example: A simple composition of an assortment makes a dramatic statement in an entryway.

hint

To assemble your own collection with very little investment, a great place to start is the church charity thrift store, where vintage crucifixes can be found for as little as a few bucks (but this isn't the place to haggle—just pay the asking price tag and smile; it's better karma).

displaying your treasures

PARE IT DOWN Start by paring down your collection. Be disciplined and choose only the best, most unique pieces—more is not always more. Giving objects room to "breathe" showcases them in a more dramatic way, making them feel more important. Believe me, I know how hard it is to keep from turning into a full-on hoarder, but resist the urge.

AVOID DUPLICATES Unless we're talking about dishes, or a matching set, it's more visually interesting to mix up several types of the same thing from different sources. If you're gathering scales, find different shapes to complement one another.

If you're collecting salt and pepper shakers, don't buy two of the same set. The less predictable, the more unique.

LOOK FOR UNIFYING DETAILS With many collections, it's the form itself that unifies them. Vintage cameras, for instance, typically look great together regardless of what combination you display them in. But a stack of linens may require a broader look at their unifying characteristics before grouping them. For interest, first try finding their commonalities—like similar color palettes or patterns from the same era.

hint

The best source for all things flea:
Walworth County flea market (just a
stone's throw from camp).

mended, baked,
scrubbed with love

As we continued to dig out yet more objects from crevices and crawl spaces, I started to realize that of all the antiques, it was the tools used for housework that had changed the least. (Have they ever invented a better flyswatter?) It's still the everyday tasks—ironing, gardening, mending, baking, cleaning—that are forgotten before they are even finished. And along with the tasks, the tools used to complete them. This is why it was so surprising to find some of the more obscure tools of the housework trade.

When we found the little vintage box of old-school wooden clothespins, I couldn't help but wonder how long it had been since they had seen a drying line (by the looks of it, not since the Kennedy administration). So it was high time that they were reincarnated. As quickly as they were found, they became the means to display photos of loved ones. We found inspiration in the everyday: apothecary jars were repurposed as cotton ball canisters, watering cans became pots for plants, milk bottles became vases. Everything we found spoke of its humble origins. So when it came time to choose what their new life would be, we stayed true to that past by using them for modest household tasks. We discovered that ladies had two types of aprons: the

OPPOSITE In a hatbox on a shelf at the back of a closet we found a box containing a small stack of hand-embroidered hankies (likely the owner's). Another fun display idea to try out: a handkerchief in one of those premade album cover frames (they are the same size as a standard hankie). The final product? Instant wall art.

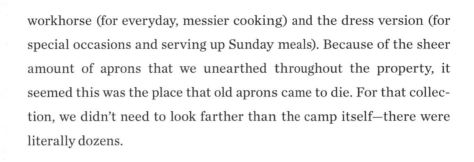

workhorse (for everyday, messier cooking) and the dress version (for special occasions and serving up Sunday meals). Because of the sheer amount of aprons that we unearthed throughout the property, it seemed this was the place that old aprons came to die. For that collection, we didn't need to look farther than the camp itself—there were literally dozens.

APRONS AREN'T JUST FOR JUNE CLEAVER ANYMORE

Who doesn't love a pretty apron? It says "cottage" like nothing else, and is the quickest way to channel your grandmother. Whenever we have houseguests, we tie one on to whomever comes within fifteen feet of the kitchen to help with breakfast.

OPPOSITE Our friend Jane drew the shortest straw and got the task of the apron cleaning. (We do this once a year as part of our spring-cleaning ritual).

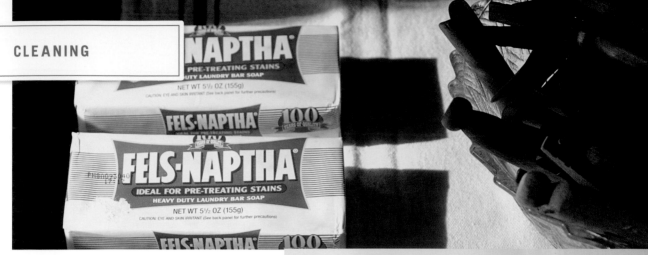

chore attire

Most women who lived in the country made their aprons from cotton and linen for house chores . . . and sometimes from the occasional feed and flour sacks for the heavier job of tending the livestock and garden work. After WWII, the idyllic home life of suburbia brought about decorative versions of aprons, with gingham, pretty trims, pockets, and unique silhouettes.

My grandmother, like most, had an arsenal of aprons, in a range of colors to match whatever outfit she donned for the day, with options to match the seasons and holidays. Because they were once so common, they are now easy to find to build a collection.

ONE BUSHEL
SEED CORN
NET WT. 56 LBS.

Genuine
PFISTER HYBRIDS
TRADE MARK REGISTERED

GROWN FROM GENUINE
PFISTER INBRED AND
FOUNDATION SEED LINES.

PFISTER ASSOCIATED GROWERS, INC.

ROLLAND MYERS
FAYETTE, OHIO.
R. F. D. 1

Doughboy
FEEDS
44

LONG LIVE THE FEED SACK

A few remnants of feed sacks in the basement, holding random odds and ends, sparked an interest to dig deeper into who used them, why, and how: Toward the end of the eighteenth century, heavy-duty cotton sacks replaced barrels for everything from livestock feed to flour. Women of the household would repurpose the flour-sack fabric to make a range of things, from rag rugs to aprons to undergarments for their farming husbands.

Today, crafting with vintage flour sacks is a popular hobby, including making clothing like they did back in WWII, when many had no other choice . . . as did my great-grandmother on my father's side.

RETRO APOTHECARY

Stocking your medicine cabinet like a vintage apothecary makes a nice surprise for houseguests digging for cotton balls. My favorite bath product that isn't actually antique but hasn't changed in over 600 years: Marseille soap (opposite, below).

RIGHT Vintage medicine jars get repurposed to store Q-tips, cotton balls, and cleaners, keeping them close at hand on a bathroom shelf. We found old jars and whiskey bottles in the chamber beneath the lodge living room (the space was used during prohibition to hide booze, no doubt).

history

I recently learned that Johnson's Baby Powder had been distributed in tins from 1893 up to 1963, then the company started using plastic containers.

ABOVE The collection of antique tins I have here (on display in a bathroom countertop) date back from the turn of the century to the sixties. It's common to find vintage tins (coffee cans being one of the most popular) in old houses, used for everything from storing bolts to burying the family's pet bird.

the lore of the tomato pincushion

ABOVE We found no shortage of tomatoes at Camp Wandawega. Apparently, it was common to bring mini sewing kits to a summer retreat, and I found tiny pincushions in several rooms. I started to collect and display them in my favorite fallback container: an oversized Ball jar.

The most popular design for a pincushion today is still the tomato with the little attached strawberry (some say it was introduced during the Victorian era). Back then, the tomato itself would have contained wool roving (to keep pins from rusting) and the strawberry was packed with an abrasive material to keep the pins clean and sharp.

Legend had it that putting a tomato in the entrance area of a home brought prosperity. Since tomatoes weren't available year round, some people resorted to making fake ones out of red cloth stuffed with hay. These would eventually serve a dual purpose as pin cushions.

A FUN LITTLE PROJECT

Instead of tossing scrap rope, twine, string, and yarn, roll them together into little balls (like the ones shown here) and create a sewing room vignette. It's free, easy, fast, and adorable on a bedside table.

ONE SERIOUSLY BIG PROJECT

Cawker City, Kansas, has the world's largest ball of twine at

- 17,980 pounds (nearly 9 tons)
- 40 feet in circumference
- 7,827,737 feet long (1,444 miles) if you were to unravel it

"Have nothing in your houses that you do not know to be useful or believe to be beautiful." —William Morris

Sewing spindles are a cottage decorator's best friend—they can be reincarnated as coat hooks, yarn storage, or candle bases, and they supply endless charm with their worn patina, wherever you display them.

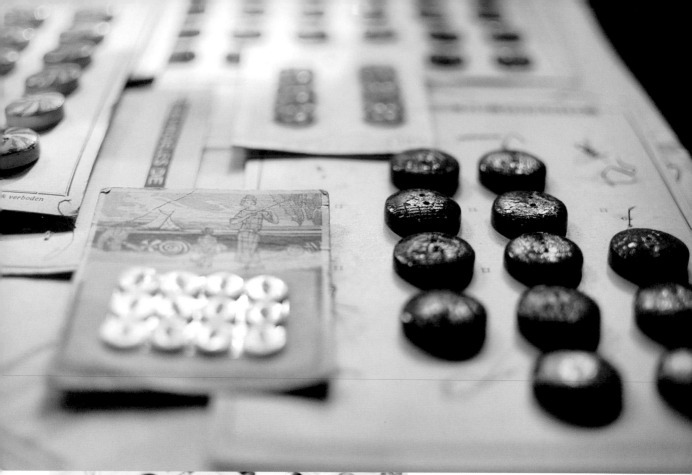

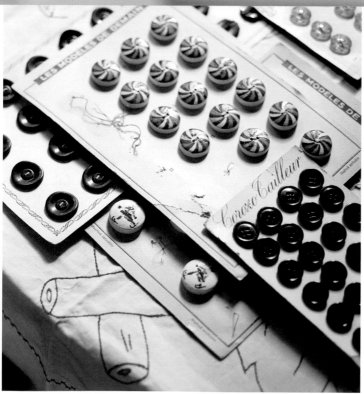

PRETTY LITTLE THINGS

Vintage button cards are quaint set out on a side table, tacked up to a bulletin board, or displayed on a clipboard in a linen, sewing, or crafts room. After finding jars of buttons around the property, I picked up these button cards at a Paris flea market. (Yes, I cheated—they didn't come from Wisconsin, but they did follow my "found, free, or flea" rule. And look how lovely they are!)

BUTTONS BY THE NUMBERS

3,000	National Button Society members
4	number of continents NBS is in
1938	the year NBS was founded
1853	the year Charles Dickens wrote an article about button making
1	the number of centimeters a button needs to fall under to be classified in the "Diminutives" category
6	the average number of buttons a zoot suit jacket has
14	the century that the game Eye Button became popular—the activity consisted of shoving buttons into each other's eyes and seeing who could hold them there the longest
147	my guesstimate of the number of buttons present in the jar shown in this photo
17,000	dollar amount that a button collection was once listed for on eBay

here and abroad

Somebody asked me once what's the point in hitting so many flea markets in so many different places, when it's easier to source things at one nearest to home (and not deal with shipping nightmares). My personal experience is that fleas are as varied and unique as the states and countries that house them—each boasting distinctively different offerings. This is just the tip of the flea iceberg, but here's a shortlist of my faves:

NEW YORK FLEAS Some of the best art books, furs, and artwork I've found were sourced in Manhattan. My hypothesis is that smaller living quarters required folks to invest more into smaller quality items. So if you're near NYC and in the market for crystal candlesticks, you won't have to look far.

WISCONSIN/ILLINOIS/MIDWEST FLEAS If you're searching for large farm implements, look no further. People have more land that they (or

their ancestors) likely farmed, so it's easy to source everything from wagon wheels to butter churns.

MINNESOTA MARKETS As you'd expect, this state is overflowing with all things "lodge." It's a haven for fishing, hunting, and trapping. One great Minnesota flea market expedition can send you home with everything from snowshoes to substantial antler racks, to a bearskin rug.

LOS ANGELES ANTIQUING If your love is Deco twenties–forties decor, this will be your main stop. Chrome, black lacquer, mirrored surfaces—it's a treasure trove of old-school glamour. I've literally found racks of satin sleeping gowns with matching feather-trimmed slippers at the LA fleas. Some of the country's best vintage evening gowns can be found at antique resale shops in and around LA, and along with them, retro costume jewelry.

THRIFTING OVERSEAS The *brocantes* of France offer an embarrassment of riches when it comes to silver serving ware and embroidered fine textiles. Catholic charity shops all over Ireland are overflowing with Irish linens, paper goods, and wonderful old biscuit tins. And in the Czech Republic, if you hit the right flea, you'll find mounds of oil paintings, antlers, hand-blown glassware, and pocketknives of all sizes. The antique shops lining Notting Hill, London, are great to hit when they are having sidewalk sales (go straight to the sale/clearance tables for flea prices). The Argentine fleas remind me very much of the Midwestern sort—with every manner of all things, but especially a large selection of equestrian gear. Every country features its own "local fare," so, for instance, while polo gear can be found at every corner at a Buenos Aires flea, it is much harder to find (and considerably more expensive) here in the States. I've had less luck

finding resale shops in China and Greece—where fleas appear to be a less integral part of their cultures (or it might require longer trips to dig deeper!). But like any country, thrift stores, resale shops, and flea market fare is also region specific . . . if you're in Champagne, France, you're much more likely to be able to source an antique champagne rack than if you are shopping in Nice. But good luck shipping items overseas; it's sometimes just too cost prohibitive, as I've found out the hard way. I learned to carry back items in large antique trunks that I find in whatever country I'm in, checked as airline baggage.

EBay has changed the landscape of the antique industry, making everything accessible to anyone, anywhere, at any time. But there's still nothing like the thrill of finding it on your own. So roll up your sleeves and hit a flea while on vacation!

6

COLLECTIONS

FOR

WORKING

reading, writing,
studying, tinkering

There it was—in the back of the attic, half covered by insulation, under three inches of dust. By the looks of it, it hadn't moved in several decades. . . .

It appeared to be a perfectly preserved box of books. After further inspection, we discovered that they were actually a set of mini board games disguised as books. Still in their original packaging. We couldn't help but wonder how the collection managed to find its way into the farthest corner of the attic and survive there, intact, for all these years. How often do we purchase a new item and save the box it came in? Rarely, if ever. That's exactly why it was so surprising to find other remnants of a former time not only still around but still intact. Pencil boxes, key fobs, and yardsticks were considered disposable—not the type of thing that was valued beyond their original modest function. In the basement, we found cigar boxes brimming with road maps. In the top shelf of a wardrobe, stacks of vintage sportsman magazines. It seemed everywhere we looked revealed more objects. We couldn't bring ourselves to toss, resell, or donate our finds—they felt like they belonged at the camp. So we decided, again, to start with each object, find similar ones to complete a set, and repurpose them: A series of

OPPOSITE A modest row of found vintage oil cans has become a charming (and functional) display along a windowsill.

PREVIOUS PAGE A collection of vintage motel keys rests on a handmade key board from an old hotel. We found an old-school vendor who still manufactures them today and had "Wandawega Lake Resort" key fobs custom made and numbered for each of the twenty-six guest rooms.

well-worn road maps were framed and grouped as a wall series. Those vintage fishing magazines still offered great advice and stories. . . . So we embraced them by collecting more of their kind, and by leaving a stack by the fireplace, on bedside tables, and near lodge chairs. When we found thirty years' worth of vintage postcards wrapped in twine (the size of a brick) in the back of a dresser, I divvied them up among the guest rooms, leaving a few in each dresser drawer to be found by overnight guests. These objects had beat the odds of survival by getting lost (and preserved) to the decades in remote corners, eventually to be discovered and repurposed as a collection for display—and a functional one at that.

LEFT I love shopping excursions. Here at a favorite stop, The Elegant Farmer, which is on the way to the city-wide yardsale in East Troy, Wisconsin.

OPPOSITE Our dear handsome William Golden volunteered to be the mobile bartender at a party by simply stocking the wagon with vintage coolers of beer.

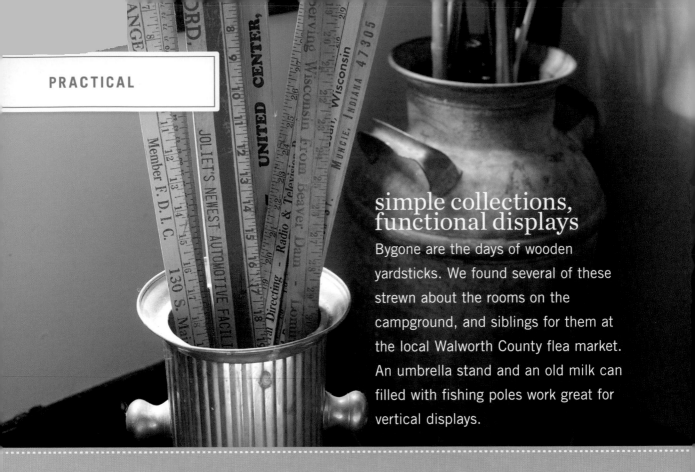

simple collections, functional displays

Bygone are the days of wooden yardsticks. We found several of these strewn about the rooms on the campground, and siblings for them at the local Walworth County flea market. An umbrella stand and an old milk can filled with fishing poles work great for vertical displays.

THE REINCARNATION OF THE APPLE CRATE

What would we do without the tried-and-true apple crate? Here are my top five uses:

1 Side table/end table/coffee table when stacked or grouped
2 Garage/basement storage (beats the pants off Rubbermaid bins)
3 Vegetable/apple barrel
4 Fall decoration display (a cute home for potted mums)
5 A carry-all for the back of the truck on flea market excursions (we always keep at least one apple crate on hand so the smaller breakable items don't roll around back there with my crazy driving)

CAMP WANDAWEGA ☀
good morning!
please stay as long as you like. And
when you are ready to depart, please
strip your sheets and leave them on your
bed, empty your trash, & sweep your floor if
you tracked anything in.
your camp counselors really appreciate
your help!! ☺

PSYCHIC SIGN-UP LIST
(ten dollar TIP contribution much appreciated)
1 6:30 — WILLIAM
2 6:45 — MATT
3 7:00 — LISA
4 7:15 — CYNDI
5 7:30 —
6 7:45 —
7 8:00 —
8 8:15 —
9 8:30 —
10 8:45 —
11 9:00 —
12 9:15 —
13 9:30 —
14 9:45 —
15 10:00 —
16 10:15 —
17 10:30 —
18 10:45 —

TO LEARN
YOUR FATE,
meet the
MEDIUM
IN THE
CANDLELIT
CHAPEL
(Follow the
Sidewalk
around to
the side
ENTRANCE)

WELCOME
to 57th ANNUAL
WANDAWEEN
12-5 — FREE-FOR-ALL (PUMPKIN' CARVIN'
SPICED CIDER, ARCHERY, CANOE'N, ETC
5-6 — GIT YUR' COSTUMES ON!
7:00 — CHILI BAR OPEN (READINGS BEGIN 6:3
8:00 — BONFIRE S'MORES (HAY RACK RIDE
10:00 — (movie projection in outdoor church)

BAR:
- Spiked Apple Cider
- Baileys & Hot Choc
- GLÜS (wine, brandy)
- Irish Coffee
- Hot Toddies

STORAGE SOLUTION

Old cigar boxes become organizers for everything from tape to ribbon. We found these all over the property and repurposed them into kitchen, bathroom, basement, and linen room organizing stacks.

HOMEMADE SIGNAGE

Chalkboards, whether the small Victorian-era slates or the sidewalk-sized easels, are great for when you entertain a large crowd and need to make guests aware of the activities of the day. They're perfect for dinner menus, drink lists, evening events, and welcome signs.

tip

Vintage fans provide unending charm, but watch out: They can also be deathtraps. Check out the cords before you plug them in—older ones often fray and could be a fire hazard. Be prepared to have them rewired if you intend on using them for extended periods of time.

scraps reincarnated as art We've literally
found cases of ephemera . . . old magazines, books, paperwork, receipts, and photographs. What doesn't get framed or archived becomes fodder for our many visiting artist friends, who welcome the opportunity to work vintage images and typography into their journals, scrapbooks, and collage artwork.

GOD SAVE THE QUEEN. AND THE PENCIL BOXES.
Nobody ever saves the lowly pencil box. Along with most office supply containers, they get tossed, but the graphics on these boxes are gorgeous, and become an installation in their own right when simply laid in a row on a desktop.

HAVE JOURNALS, WILL TRAVEL

Don't scrap the photo books. Photo albums today don't have the same charm as their old-school counterparts. I've been collecting vintage unused (aka new old stock) scrapbooks, journals, and photo albums since high school. They require more effort to assemble (with photo corners or glue), but it is a labor of love. And what you end up with is a lovely collection of your travels, stories, and memories as a keepsake to relive and an heirloom to leave for your children. A stack of them on a side table becomes a welcome invitation to kick back with a cup of coffee and take a trip.

ABOVE A new idea for displaying your favorite collectible postcards: an antique discarded hymnal rack from a church (you can also use them as book racks). We keep ours in the main lodge to greet guests and fill it with antique postcards from the local Wisconsin area.

LEFT Whether tacked to a bulletin board, sewn to a bedspread, or upholstered on a vintage tartan throw, letterman letter patches are hard to find, sometimes expensive, but always charming. I've been collecting these for some time, but have yet to decide which installation I'd like to commit them all to.

ABOVE AND RIGHT Two of the more common preassembled collections you can find at flea markets: cigar labels and stamps.

14 ISSUES $2.92   14 ISSUES $2.34   52 ISSUES $3.88   12 ISSUES $2.50

12 ISSUES $2.50   30 ISSUES $2.98   16 ISSUES $2.50   12 ISSUES $2.00

23 ISSUES $2.88   23 ISSUES $2.88   23 ISSUES $1.97

BOOKWORM

A fast, effortless collection that adds vintage allure to any room is a stack of old books. They make for great rainy-day pastimes. My favorite sources:

1 Salvation Army (or any thrift store, for that matter)
2 Estate sales
3 Yard sales/tag sales/garage sales
4 Library "old stock" sales
5 Auctions (a great place to find boxes of books that you can buy in a single lot)
6 Your great-aunt's attic/basement/bookshelf (she'll probably be happy to pass them on to a good home)

OLD-SCHOOL SCRAPBOOKING

This is not your mom's "scrapbook" hobby that has
become all the rage. Try a different, truly custom
approach. I like to call it evolved journaling, where I
start with an antique unused photo album and fill
each page with mini installations using only vintage
ephemera. The final result is a beautiful, antique
collection of objects to be found nowhere else.

VINTAGE MAPS—HOW DO I LOVE THEE?

Let me count the ways:

1 as a decoupage under a glass-top table
2 as a wallpaper collage in a small closet or bath
3 as a surprise find in guest room drawers
4 as a cheap source of entertainment (looking for what's changed on our favorite road trips)

"It is perhaps a more fortunate destiny to have a taste for collecting shells than to be born a millionaire."

—Robert Louis Stevenson

ABOVE We found this box of maps at a rural yardsale. At fifty cents a pop, we walked away with an entire collection for about five bucks. (That wouldn't even cover the shipping if we'd have bought them on eBay.)

SMALL PACKAGES, BIG CHARM.
Don't overlook the details. This
antique painter's palette is the
perfect foundation for a small
collection of paint blocks. It serves
as an easy tabletop vignette for the
artist's studio at the camp.

PATCHES REINCARNATED INTO WALL ART

If you've got the patience, you can turn an old collection of Boy Scout patches into wall art.

STEP 1: Find an old frame that is the approximate scale to house your display.

STEP 2: Cut a board to fit the frame, wrap it in fabric (staple-gun it to the back side).

STEP 3: Affix the patches (with a hot glue gun and pins) to the board.

STEP 4: Screw the frame into the finished board and hang! Admire your fabulous creation.

on the cheap

FOUND Search the newspapers for listings of spring clean-up days. (Going for the nice neighborhoods is always your best bet for better finds.) Start with drive-bys to see what there may be curbside. Most folks will leave unwanted pieces right by the street.

FREE Put the word out. Some folks are willing to give away old furniture and books to anyone willing to simply cart it away for them (especially big items like sofas and pianos that are hard to move). Craigslist is a good source to find folks who are moving and looking to unload objects quickly.

FLEA Flea markets are a tried-and-true source for all the best finds. TIP: If you visit late in the day (an hour before close is the best time), vendors will be packing up their wares and willing to deal in order to avoid carting it all back home. Don't be afraid to haggle; they're typically willing to negotiate late in the day.

and . . . Don't forget the church tag sales, garage sales, barn sales, estate sales, moving sales, fire sales, charity shops, thrift stores, resale shops, consignment shops. . . . If you're open to digging a bit, it's always worth the trouble. Some of the best deals and steals can be found in these places.

epilogue

I remember an antiques dealer once saying that she liked to walk into a room full of her favorite antiques and imagine being greeted by the good-karma ghosts of original owners of each of the items—those souls who at one time cherished or relied on each of those objects. I'd like to think that a bit of the residual goodwill of each prior owner might still be left with the items we've found here at the camp during our six-year-long resurrection. Hopefully they would be happy to know that their beloved quilt or teapot or watering can has a new, useful life in the same place in which it was found.

So the next time you think you might need something for the house, consider first rescuing it from your local thrift store, charity shop, yard sale, or Grandma's attic. If you stick with the "found, free, or flea" mantra, you'll save money and somebody's once-precious "something." And best of all, you'll get the bonus good feeling of knowing that you saved a relic that might have been destined for the trash bin.

Thriftiness and determination can transform any forgotten item into a collection. I find that at the end of the day, if we surround ourselves with "lost" objects and embrace their individual stories—and incorporate them into our lives and homes—it brings our surroundings much more depth and richness.

Here's to finding the little stories. Happy hunting!

acknowledgments

Thank you to:

Andy Barzvi for being such a rock star agent. Angelin Borsics for her never-ending patience and editing superpowers. Stephanie Huntwork for her great eye and talent, and the rest of the Clarkson Potter team for their support. Special thanks to Herb and Anna for bringing David into the world and for introducing him to this magical little place you call "Vandavega." For all our friends (too many to list) who have shared this place with us, helping us year after year. My brother Sam and his crew of treemen who keep coming back to keep it safe for everyone. A lifetime of thank-yous to all who envisioned and erected "Tom's treehouse" . . . Angela, Bladdon, Steven, and their extended crew . . . and most especially, the incredible "Stone Blitzer"—Shaun and Tyler for their endless generosity of time and talent to make it happen. Sandy Possati and her family for so generously allowing us to use her family photos, for coming to visit us at Wandawega Lake Resort, and for sharing stories of parents and grandparents who gave so much life and history to this place.

To David for continuing to put up with me, and to Frankie for finding his way to us.

And to CHARLIE . . . who we cannot wait to share this place with.

Every collection, photo, and room in this
book is from our summer retreat,
Wandawega Lake Resort. To learn more or
to pay us a visit, go to wandawega.com.

photo credits

VINCE COOK
vincecookphotography.com
94 (center), 116, 117 (top right), 199

AIMEE HERRING
aimeeherringphotography.com
98

BOB COSCARELLI
bobcoscarelli.com
2, 6 (top left), 23, 26 (bottom), 42 (top), 43
(bottom and second from bottom), 67, 73,
92-93, 99, 100, 102, 103, 108, 119 (top), 181,
200-201, 204 (top)

JULIA STOTZ
juliastotz.com
7 (bottom left and center right), 20-21, 28 (top and
bottom right), 29, 30-31, 34, 35, 43 (top right), 46
(top), 48, 54 (bottom), 55 (top left and bottom), 56, 57
(top), 58, 66, 74, 81, 112 (bottom), 121 (left), 155 (top
right),165 (top), 166, 168-169, 171, 177, 180 (top),
184, 185, 186, 197 (bottom)

DAVID ROBERT ELLIOTT
davidrobertelliott.com
6 (bottom right), 55 (top right), 127, 139
(bottom), 145 (top), 147, 155 (bottom), 159, 180
(bottom), 187 (bottom)

CHRIS STRONG
chrisstrongphotography.com
12 (bottom left), 45, 50-51, 70, 80 (top and bottom),
94 (bottom), 189 (bottom)

GREG GILLIS
greggillisphotography.com
208

BJORN WALLANDER
bjornwallander.com
149, 178, 179, 182

MATT GORE
matthewgore.com
4-5, 7 (bottom right), 12 (top right), 13 (center left,
top right, and bottom right), 26 (top), 27, 32-33, 37
(top), 38, 39, 43 (second from top), 44, 46 (bottom),
49, 52, 54 (top), 57 (bottom), 59, 60, 61 (top), 62-63,
64, 69, 71, 72, 75, 76 (right), 77, 78 (bottom), 79, 80
(center), 83, 86-87, 89 (top), 96, 97, 101, 104, 106,
107, 109 (bottom), 113, 119 (bottom), 120, 122-123,
126 (bottom), 130 (top), 134, 135 (bottom), 137, 138,
139 (top), 140-141, 142-143, 145 (bottom), 157, 160,
164, 165 (bottom), 170, 175, 183 (bottom), 187 (top),
188-189, 190-191, 192, 194, 195, 197 (top), 204
(bottom right), 205, 207

TEREASA SURRATT
notaphotographer.com
6 (center and bottom left), 7 (top left and right), 12 (top
left, center left, center, and bottom left), 13 (bottom
left and center right), 18-19, 28 (top left), 37 (bottom),
40-41, 47 (top), 61 (bottom), 76 (left), 84-85, 89
(bottom), 94 (top left and right), 105, 109 (top left and
right), 110, 111, 114, 115, 117 (top left and bottom), 118,
121 (right), 124, 125, 126 (top), 130 (bottom), 131, 135
(top), 136, 155 (top left), 156, 162, 163, 167, 174 (top),
183 (top), 193, 204 (bottom left)

**Antique photographs courtesy of Father
Baginskis and Sandy Possati.**

JACOB HAND
jacobhand.com
10, 13 (top left), 24, 36, 42 (bottom), 47 (bottom),
53, 78 (top), 90, 95, 100, 112 (top), 133, 144,
148, 150, 151, 152, 153, 174 (bottom), 203

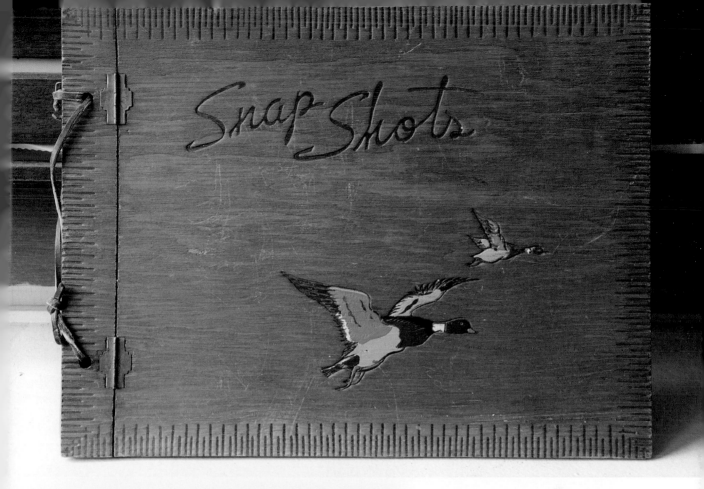

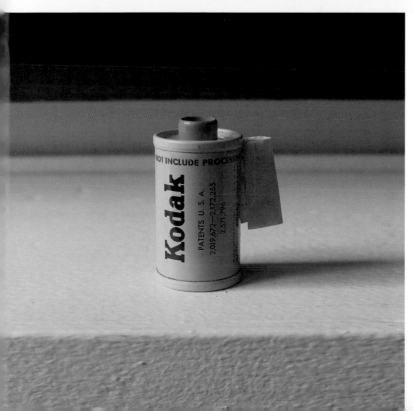

This book was made possible by the generosity of our talented photographer comrades. Thanks a bazillion for your friendship and photographs. Wanda's door is always open to you.

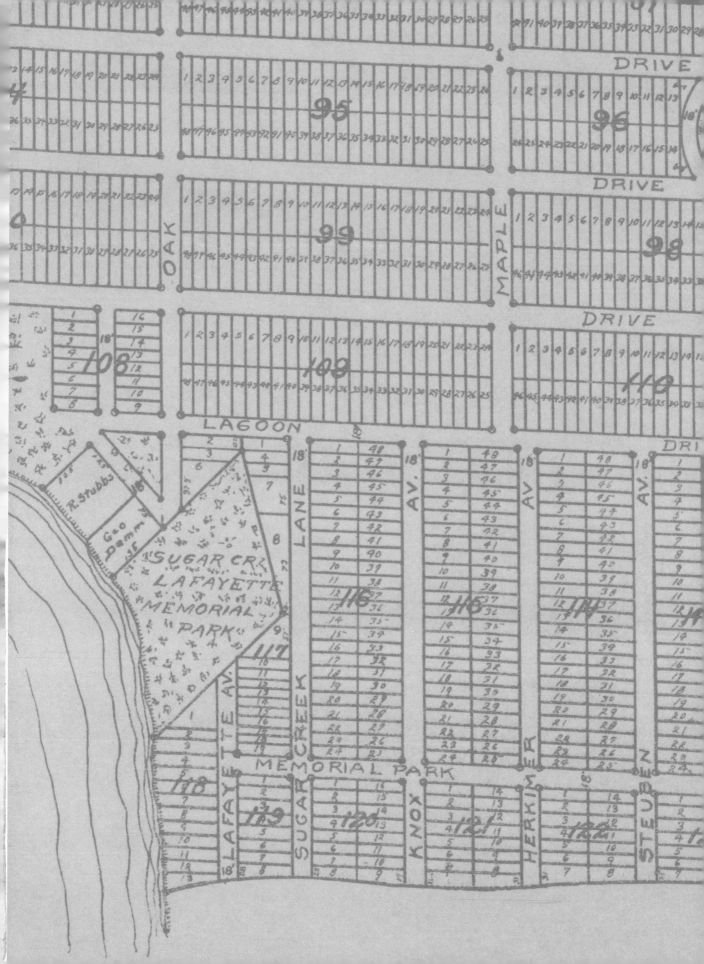

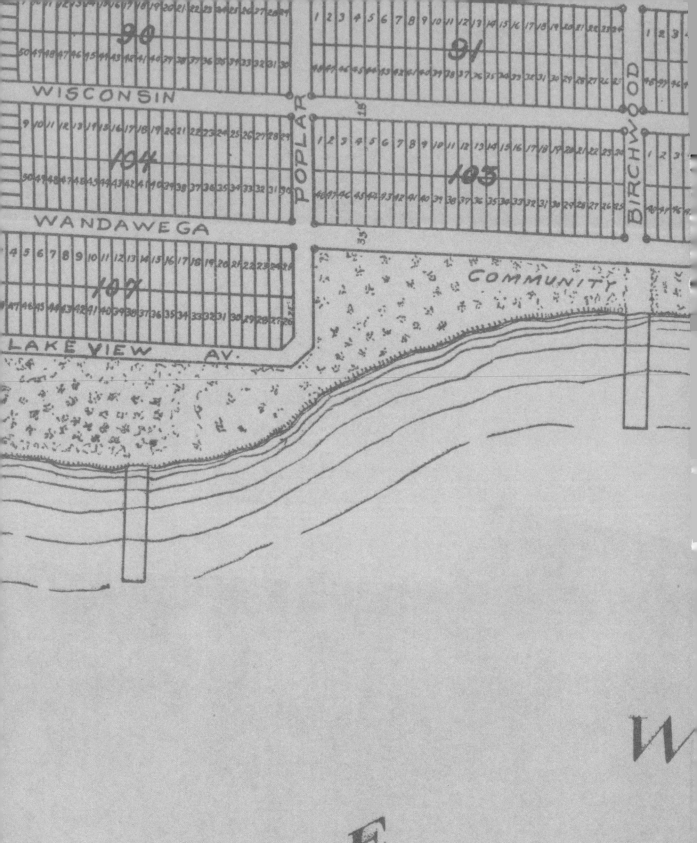

WISCONSIN

WANDAWEGA

LAKE VIEW AV.

POPLAR

BIRCHWOOD

COMMUNITY

L A K E